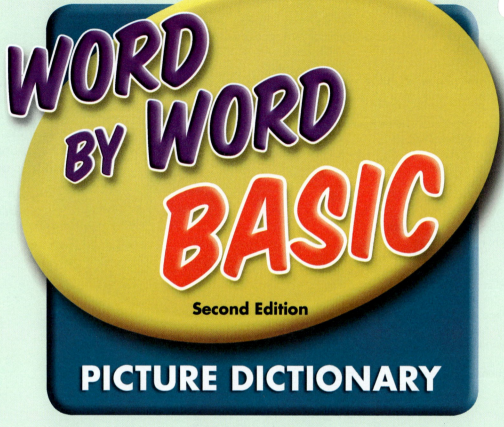

WORD BY WORD BASIC

Second Edition

PICTURE DICTIONARY

Steven J. Molinsky • Bill Bliss

Illustrated by
Richard E. Hill

longman.com

Word by Word Basic Picture Dictionary, second edition

Pearson Education, 10 Bank Street, White Plains, NY 10606

Editorial director: Pam Fishman
Vice president, director of design and production: Rhea Banker
Director of electronic production: Aliza Greenblatt
Director of manufacturing: Patrice Fraccio
Senior manufacturing manager: Edith Pullman
Director of marketing: Oliva Fernandez
Senior digital layout specialist: Wendy Wolf
Text design: Wendy Wolf
Cover design: Tracey Munz Cataldo/Warren Fischbach
Realia creation: Warren Fischbach, Paula Williams
Illustrations: Richard E. Hill
Contributing artists: Steven Young, Charles Cawley, Willard Gage, Marlon Violette
WordSongs Music CD: Peter S. Bliss

Additional photos/illustration: Page **244** *top* U.S. National Archives & Records Administration

Library of Congress Cataloging-in-Publication Data
Molinsky, Steven J.
  Word by word basic picture dictionary / Steven J. Molinsky, Bill Bliss.—2nd ed.
     p. cm.
  Includes index.
  ISBN 0-13-148225-4
1. Picture dictionaries, English. 2. English language—Textbooks for foreign speakers. I. Bliss, Bill. II. Title.
PE1629.M582 2006
423'.17--dc22

                          2005044359

ISBN 0-13-207874-0; 978-0-13-207874-0
Longman on the Web
Longman.com offers online resources for teachers and students. Access our Companion Websites,
our online catalog, and our local offices around the world.

Visit us at longman.com.

Printed in the United States of America
2 3 4 5 6 7 8 9 10 – RRD – 11 10 09 08

Dedicated to Janet Johnston in honor of her wonderful contribution to the development of our textbooks over three decades.

Steven J. Molinsky
Bill Bliss

CONTENTS

Unit / Theme	Communication Skills	Writing & Discussion	CASAS	LAUSD	LCPs
1 **Personal Information and Family**	• Asking for & giving personal information • Identifying information on a form • Spelling name aloud • Identifying family members • Introducing others	• Telling about yourself • Telling about family members • Drawing a family tree	0.1.2, 0.1.4, 0.2.1, 0.2.2	*Beg. Literacy:* 1, 2, 3, 4, 5 *Beg. Low:* 1, 2, 4, 6, 7, 9, 58 *Beg. High:* 1, 4, 5, 6	*Literacy LCPs:* 01, 02, 07, 08, 15, 16 *LCP A:* 05, 14, 15 *LCP B:* 22, 31 *LCP C:* 39
2 **At School**	• Identifying classroom objects • Identifying classroom locations • Identifying classroom actions • Giving & following simple classroom commands • Identifying school locations & personnel	• Describing a classroom • Describing a school • Comparing schools in different countries	0.1.2, 0.1.5	*Beg. Literacy:* 8, 9, 11 *Beg. Low:* 12, 13, 15, 16, 17, 18 *Beg. High:* 12, 14, 15	*Literacy LCPs:* 01, 07, 15
3 **Common Everyday Activities and Language**	• Identifying everyday & leisure activities • Inquiring by phone about a person's activities • Asking about a person's plan for future activities • Social communication: Greeting people, Leave taking, Introducing yourself & others, Getting someone's attention, Expressing gratitude, Saying you don't understand, Calling someone on the telephone • Describing the weather • Interpreting temperatures on a thermometer (Fahrenheit & Centigrade) • Describing the weather forecast for tomorrow	• Making a list of daily activities • Describing daily routine • Making a list of planned activities • Describing favorite leisure activities • Describing the weather	0.1.1, 0.1.2, 0.1.4, 0.1.6, 0.2.1, 0.2.4, 1.1.5, 2.1.8, 2.3.3, 7.5.5, 7.5.6, 8.2.3, 8.2.5	*Beg. Literacy:* 5, 6 *Beg. Low:* 9, 11, 12, 13, 28, 29 *Beg. High:* 7a, 7b, 11, 26	*Literacy LCPs:* 01, 02, 07, 08, 15, 16 *LCP A:* 05, 06, 13 *LCP B:* 22, 30 *LCP C:* 39, 47

CASAS: Comprehensive Adult Student Assessment System
LAUSD: Los Angeles Unified School District content standards *(Beginning Literacy, Beginning Low, Beginning High)*
LCPs: Literacy Completion Points – Florida & Texas workforce development skills & life skills –
    (Literacy levels; LCP A – Literacy/Foundations; LCP B – Low Beginning; LCP C – High Beginning)

Unit / Theme	Communication Skills	Writing & Discussion	CASAS	LAUSD	LCPs
4 Numbers/ Time/ Money/ Calendar	• Using cardinal & ordinal numbers • Giving information about age, number of family members, residence • Telling time • Indicating time of events • Asking for information about arrival & departure times • Identifying coins & currency – names & values • Making & asking for change • Identifying days of the week • Identifying months of the year • Asking about the year, month, day, date • Asking about the date of a birthday, anniversary, appointment • Giving date of birth	• Describing numbers of students in a class • Identifying a country's population • Describing daily schedule with times • Telling about the use of time in different cultures or countries • Describing the cost of purchases • Describing coins & currency of other countries • Describing weekday activities • Telling about favorite day of the week & month of the year	0.1.2, 0.2.1, 1.1.6, 2.3.1, 2.3.2	*Beg. Literacy:* 6, 12, 13 *Beg. Low:* 3, 4, 25, 26, 30 *Beg. High:* 2, 5	*Literacy LCPs:* 01, 03, 07, 09, 15, 17 *LCP A:* 08 *LCP B:* 25 *LCP C:* 42
5 Home	• Identifying types of housing & communities • Requesting a taxi • Calling 911 for an ambulance • Identifying rooms of a home • Identifying furniture • Complimenting • Asking for information in a store • Locating items in a store • Asking about items on sale • Asking the location of items at home • Telling about past weekend activities • Identifying locations in an apartment building • Identifying ways to look for housing: classified ads, listings, vacancy signs • Renting an apartment • Describing household problems • Securing home repair services • Making a suggestion • Identifying household cleaning items • Identifying tools and home supplies • Asking to borrow an item	• Describing types of housing where people live • Describing rooms & furniture in a residence • Telling about baby products & early child-rearing practices in different countries • Telling about personal experiences with repairing things • Describing an apartment building • Describing household cleaning chores	0.1.2, 0.1.4, 1.4.1, 1.4.2, 1.4.7, 2.1.2, 7.5.5, 8.2.5, 8.2.6	*Beg. Low:* 12, 13, 21, 38, 39 *Beg. High:* 10c, 20, 37, 38, 39	*Literacy LCPs:* 01, 07, 11, 15, 19 *LCP A:* 04, 06, 11 *LCP B:* 21 *LCP C:* 38, 40, 45
6 Community	• Identifying places in the community • Exchanging greetings • Asking & giving the location of places in the community • Identifying government buildings, services, & other places in a city/town center • Identifying modes of transportation in a city/town center	• Describing places in a neighborhood • Making a list of places, people, & actions observed at an intersection	0.1.2, 0.1.4, 2.5.3, 2.5.4	*Beg. Literacy:* 5, 11 *Beg. Low:* 22, 23, 24 *Beg. High:* 23	*Literacy LCPs:* 01, 04, 07, 11, 15 *LCP A:* 05, 12 *LCP B:* 29 *LCP C:* 46

Unit / Theme	Communication Skills	Writing & Discussion	CASAS	LAUSD	LCPs
7 **Describing**	• Describing people by age • Describing people by physical characteristics • Describing a suspect or missing person to a police officer • Describing people & things using adjectives • Describing physical states & emotions • Expressing concern about another person's physical state or emotion	• Describing physical characteristics of yourself & family members • Describing physical characteristics of a favorite actor or actress or other famous person • Describing things at home & in the community • Telling about personal experiences with different emotions	0.1.2, 0.2.1	*Beg. Literacy:* 7 *Beg. Low:* 6 *Beg. High:* 3, 7b	*Literacy LCPs:* 01, 07, 15 *LCP A:* 05 *LCP B:* 22 *LCP C:* 39, 49
8 **Food**	• Identifying food items (fruits, vegetables, meat, poultry, seafood, dairy products, juices, beverages, deli, frozen foods, snack foods, groceries) • Identifying non-food items purchased in a supermarket (e.g., household supplies, baby products, pet food) • Determining food needs to make a shopping list • Asking the location of items in a supermarket • Identifying supermarket sections • Requesting items at a service counter in a supermarket • Identifying supermarket checkout area personnel & items • Identifying food containers & quantities • Identifying units of measure • Asking for & giving recipe instructions • Complimenting someone on a recipe • Offering to help with food preparation • Identifying food preparation actions • Ordering fast food items, coffee shop items, & sandwiches • Indicating a shortage of supplies to a co-worker or supervisor • Taking customers' orders at a food service counter • Identifying restaurant objects, personnel, & actions • Making & following requests at work • Identifying & correctly positioning silverware & plates in a table setting • Inquiring in person about restaurant job openings • Ordering from a restaurant menu • Taking customers' orders as a waiter or waitress in a restaurant	• Describing favorite & least favorite foods • Describing foods in different countries • Making a shopping list • Describing places to shop for food • Telling about differences between supermarkets & food stores in different countries • Making a list of items in kitchen cabinets & the refrigerator • Describing recycling practices • Describing a favorite recipe using units of measure • Telling about experience with different types of restaurants • Describing restaurants and menus in different countries • Describing favorite foods ordered in restaurants	0.1.2, 0.1.4, 1.1.1, 1.1.7, 1.3.7, 1.3.8, 2.6.4, 4.8.3	*Beg. Literacy:* 5, 14 *Beg. Low:* 14, 32, 35, 37 *Beg. High:* 10c, 30, 31, 34, 36	*Literacy LCPs:* 01, 05, 07, 12, 15, 20 *LCP A:* 05, 07, 11 *LCP B:* 24, 28 *LCP C:* 45

Unit / Theme	Communication Skills	Writing & Discussion	CASAS	LAUSD	LCPs
9 **Colors, Clothing, & Shopping**	• Identifying colors • Complimenting someone on clothing • Identifying clothing items, including outerwear, sleepwear, underwear, exercise clothing, footwear, jewelry, & accessories • Talking about appropriate clothing for different weather conditions • Expressing clothing needs to a store salesperson • Locating clothing items • Inquiring about ownership of found clothing items • Indicating loss of a clothing item • Asking about sale prices in a clothing store • Reporting theft of a clothing item to the police • Stating preferences during clothing shopping • Expressing problems with clothing & the need for alterations • Identifying departments & services in a department store • Asking the location of items in a department store • Asking to buy, return, exchange, try on, & pay for department store items • Asking about regular & sales prices, discounts, & sales tax • Interpreting a sales receipt • Offering assistance to customers as a salesperson • Expressing needs to a salesperson in a store • Identifying electronics products, including video & audio equipment, telephones, cameras, & computers • Identifying components of a computer & common computer software • Complimenting someone about an item & inquiring where it was purchased	• Describing the flags of different countries • Telling about emotions associated with different colors • Telling about clothing & colors you like to wear • Describing clothing worn at different occasions (e.g., going to schools, parties, weddings) • Telling about clothing worn in different weather conditions • Telling about clothing worn during exercise activities • Telling about footwear worn during different activities • Describing the color, size, & pattern of favorite clothing items • Comparing clothing fashions now & a long time ago • Describing a department store • Telling about stores that have sales • Telling about an item purchased on sale • Comparing different types & brands of video & audio equipment, telephones, & cameras • Describing personal use of a computer • Sharing opinions about why computers are important	0.1.2, 0.1.3, 0.1.4, 1.1.9, 1.2.1, 1.2.2, 1.2.3, 1.3.3, 1.3.7, 1.3.9, 1.6.3, 1.6.4, 4.8.3, 8.2.4	*Beg. Literacy:* 5, 8, 13, 14 *Beg. Low:* 14, 31, 32, 33, 34 *Beg. High:* 10c, 30, 33, 60	*Literacy LCPs:* 01, 04, 07, 11, 15, 19 *LCP A:* 05, 11, 15 *LCP B:* 28 *LCP C:* 45

Unit / Theme	Communication Skills	Writing & Discussion	CASAS	LAUSD	LCPs
10 **Community Services**	• Requesting bank services & transactions (e.g., deposit, withdrawal, cashing a check, obtaining traveler's checks, opening an account, applying for a loan, exchanging currency) • Identifying bank personnel • Identifying bank forms • Asking about acceptable forms of payment (cash, check, credit card, money order, traveler's check) • Identifying household bills (rent, utilities, etc.) • Identifying family finance documents & actions • Following instructions to use an ATM machine • Requesting post office services & transactions • Identifying types of mail & mail services • Identifying different ways to buy stamps • Requesting non-mail services available at the post office (money order, selective service registration, passport application) • Identifying & locating library sections, services, & personnel • Asking how to find a book in the library • Identifying community institutions, services, and personnel (police, fire, city government, public works, recreation, sanitation, religious institutions) • Identifying types of emergency vehicles	• Describing use of bank services • Telling about household bills & amounts paid • Telling about the person responsible for household finances • Describing use of ATM machines • Describing use of postal services • Comparing postal systems in different countries • Telling about experience using a library • Telling about the location of community institutions • Describing experiences using community institutions	0.1.2, 1.3.1, 1.3.3, 1.4.4, 1.5.1, 1.5.3, 1.8.1, 1.8.2, 1.8.4, 2.4.1, 2.4.2, 2.4.4, 2.5.1, 2.5.4, 2.5.6, 8.2.1	*Beg. Low:* 8 *Beg. High:* 24, 28, 29	*Literacy LCPs:* 01, 07, 15, 19 *LCP A:* 08, 11, 12 *LCP B:* 25, 28, 29 *LCP C:* 42, 44, 46

Unit / Theme	Communication Skills	Writing & Discussion	CASAS	LAUSD	LCPs
11 Health	• Identifying parts of the body & key internal organs • Describing ailments, symptoms, & injuries • Asking about the health of another person • Identifying items in a first-aid kit • Describing medical emergencies • Identifying emergency medical procedures (CPR, rescue breathing, Heimlich maneuver) • Calling 911 to report a medical emergency • Identifying major illnesses • Talking with a friend or co-worker about illness in one's family • Following instructions during a medical examination • Identifying medical personnel, equipment, & supplies in medical & dental offices • Understanding medical & dental personnel's description of procedures during treatment • Understanding a doctor's medical advice and instructions • Identifying over-the-counter medications • Understanding dosage instructions on medicine labels • Identifying hospital departments & personnel • Identifying equipment in a hospital room • Identifying actions & items related to personal hygiene • Locating personal care products in a store • Identifying actions & items related to baby care	• Describing self • Telling about a personal experience with an illness or injury • Describing remedies or treatments for common problems (cold, stomachache, insect bite, hiccups) • Describing experience with a medical emergency • Describing a medical examination • Describing experience with a medical or dental procedure • Telling about medical advice received • Telling about over-the-counter medications used • Comparing use of medications in different countries • Describing a hospital stay • Making a list of personal care items needed for a trip • Comparing baby products in different countries	0.1.2, 0.1.4, 1.3.7, 2.1.2, 2.5.3, 2.5.9, 3.1.1, 3.1.2, 3.1.3, 3.3.1, 3.3.2, 3.3.3, 3.4.2, 3.4.3, 3.5.4, 3.5.5, 3.5.9, 8.1.1	*Beg. Literacy:* 9 *Beg. Low:* 12, 21, 32, 43, 44, 45, 46 *Beg. High:* 10b, 20, 30, 43, 45, 46, 47, 50	*Literacy LCPs:* 01, 05, 06, 07, 12, 14, 15, 20, 22 *LCP A:* 06, 07, 10, 14 *LCP B:* 24, 27 *LCP C:* 40, 41, 44, 48

Unit / Theme	Communication Skills	Writing & Discussion	CASAS	LAUSD	LCPs

12 **School Subjects and Activities**	• Identifying school subjects
	• Identifying extracurricular activities
	• Sharing after-school plans
	• MATH:
	  • Asking & answering basic questions during a math class
	  • Using fractions to indicate sale prices
	  • Using percents to indicate test scores & probability in weather forecasts
	  • Identifying high school math subjects
	  • Using measurement terms to indicate height, width, depth, length, distance
	  • Interpreting metric measurements
	  • Identifying types of lines, geometric shapes, & solid figures
	• ENGLISH LANGUAGE ARTS:
	  • Identifying types of sentences
	  • Identifying parts of speech
	  • Identifying punctuation marks
	  • Providing feedback during peer-editing
	  • Identifying steps of the writing process
	  • Identifying types of literature
	  • Identifying forms of writing
	• GEOGRAPHY:
	  • Identifying geographical features & bodies of water
	  • Identifying natural environments (desert, jungle, rainforest, etc.)
	• SCIENCE:
	  • Identifying science classroom/laboratory equipment
	  • Asking about equipment needed to do a science procedure
	  • Identifying steps of the scientific method
		• Telling about favorite school subject
		• Telling about extracurricular activities
		• Comparing extracurricular activities in different countries
		• Describing math education
		• Telling about something bought on sale
		• Researching & sharing information about population statistics using percents
		• Describing favorite books & authors
		• Describing newspapers & magazines read
		• Telling about use of different types of written communication
		• Describing the geography of your country
		• Describing geographical features experienced
		• Describing experience with scientific equipment
		• Describing science education
		• Brainstorming a science experiment & describing each step of the scientific method
			0.1.2,
			0.1.3,
			0.1.5,
			0.2.3,
			1.1.2,
			1.1.4,
			2.5.5,
			2.5.9,
			2.7.5,
			5.2.5,
			6.0.1,
			6.0.2,
			6.0.4,
			6.1.1,
			6.1.2,
			6.1.3,
			6.1.4,
			6.4.1,
			6.4.2,
			6.6.1,
			6.6.2,
			6.8.1
				Beg. Literacy:
				15
				Beg. Low:
				12, 16, 17
				Beg. High:
				7a, 14, 31
					Literacy LCPs:
					01, 07, 15
					LCP A: 14
					LCP B: 31
					LCP C: 39,
					48

Unit / Theme	Communication Skills	Writing & Discussion	CASAS	LAUSD	LCPs
13 **Work**	• Identifying occupations • Talking about occupation during social conversation • Identifying job skills & work activities • Indicating job skills during an interview • Identifying types of job advertisements (help wanted signs, job notices, classified ads) • Interpreting abbreviations in job advertisements • Identifying each step in a job-search process • Making requests at work • Identifying factory locations, equipment, & personnel • Asking the location of workplace departments & personnel to orient oneself as a new employee • Asking about the location & activities of a co-worker • Identifying construction site machinery, equipment, and building materials • Asking a co-worker for a workplace item • Warning a co-worker of a safety hazard • Asking whether there is a sufficient supply of workplace materials • Identifying job safety equipment • Interpreting warning signs at work • Reminding someone to use safety equipment • Asking the location of emergency equipment at work	• Career exploration: sharing ideas about occupations that are interesting, difficult, important • Describing occupation & occupations of family members • Describing job skills • Describing a familiar job (skill requirements, qualifications, hours, salary) • Telling about how people found their jobs • Telling about experience with a job search or job interview • Describing a nearby factory & working conditions there • Comparing products produced by factories in different countries • Describing building materials used in ones dwelling • Describing a nearby construction site • Telling about experience with safety equipment • Describing the use of safety equipment in the community	0.1.2, 0.1.6, 4.1.2, 4.1.3, 4.1.5, 4.1.6, 4.1.7, 4.1.8, 4.3.1, 4.3.3, 4.3.4, 4.5.1, 4.6.1, 7.1.1, 7.5.5	*Beg. Literacy:* 5, 10 *Beg. Low:* 11, 12, 14, 48, 49, 50, 51, 52, 53, 54, 56 *Beg. High:* 7a, 8a, 11, 51, 54	*Literacy LCPs:* 01, 07, 10, 14, 15, 18, 22 *LCP A:* 01, 02, 03, 04, 10 *LCP B:* 18, 19, 20, 21, 27 *LCP C:* 35, 36, 38, 44
14 **Transportation and Travel**	• Identifying modes of local & inter-city public transportation • Expressing intended mode of travel • Asking about a location to obtain transportation (bus stop, bus station, train station, subway station) • Locating ticket counters, information booths, fare card machines, & information signage in transportation stations • Giving & following driving directions (using prepositions of motion) • Interpreting traffic signs • Warning a driver about an upcoming sign • Interpreting compass directions • Asking for driving directions • Following instructions during a driver's test • Repeating to confirm instructions • Identifying airport locations & personnel (check-in, security, gate, baggage claim, Customs & Immigration) • Asking for location of places & personnel at an airport • Indicating loss of travel documents or other items	• Describing mode of travel to different places in the community • Describing local public transportation • Comparing transportation in different countries • Describing your route from home to school • Describing how to get to different places from home and school • Describing local traffic signs • Comparing traffic signs in different countries • Describing a familiar airport • Telling about an experience with Customs & Immigration	0.1.2, 0.1.3, 0.1.6, 1.9.1, 1.9.2, 1.9.4, 2.2.1, 2.2.2, 2.2.3, 2.2.4, 2.5.4	*Beg. Literacy:* 5, 10 *Beg. Low:* 11, 13, 23, 24, 42, 48, 49 *Beg. High:* 11, 23, 41	*Literacy LCPs:* 01, 04, 06, 07, 13, 15, 21 *LCP A:* 09 *LCP B:* 26 *LCP C:* 43

Unit / Theme	Communication Skills	Writing & Discussion	CASAS	LAUSD	LCPs
15 **Recreation and Entertainment**	• Identifying places to go for outdoor recreation, entertainment, culture, etc. • Asking for & offering a suggestion for a leisure activity • Describing past weekend activities • Describing activities planned for a future day off or weekend • Identifying individual sports & recreation activities • Asking and telling about favorite sports and recreation activities • Describing exercise habits & routines • Identifying team sports & terms for players & playing fields • Commenting on a player's performance during a game • Engaging in small talk about favorite sports, teams, and players • Identifying types of entertainment & cultural events • Identifying different genres of music, movies, & TV programs • Expressing likes about types of entertainment	• Describing favorite places to go & activities there • Describing favorite individual sports & recreation activities • Comparing individual sports & recreation activities popular in different countries • Describing favorite team sports & famous players • Telling about favorite types of entertainment • Comparing types of entertainment popular in different countries • Telling about favorite performers • Telling about favorite types of music, movies, & TV programs	0.1.2, 0.1.3, 0.1.4, 0.2.4, 2.6.1, 2.6.2, 2.6.3, 2.7.6, 3.5.8, 3.5.9	*Beg. Low:* 12, 13, 14 *Beg. High:* 7a	*Literacy LCPs:* 01, 07, 15 *LCP A:* 05, 06 *LCP C:* 39
16 **U.S. Civics**	• Producing correct form of identification when requested (driver's license, social security card, student I.D. card, employee I.D. badge, permanent resident card, passport, visa, work permit, birth certificate, proof of residence) • Identifying the three branches of U.S. government (legislative, executive, judicial) & their functions • Identifying senators, representatives, the president, vice-president, cabinet, Supreme Court justices, & the chief justice, & the branches of government in which they work • Identifying the key buildings in each branch of government (Capitol Building, White House, Supreme Court Building) • Identifying the Constitution as "the supreme law of the land" • Identifying the Bill of Rights • Naming freedoms guaranteed by the 1st Amendment • Identifying key amendments to the Constitution • Identifying key holidays & dates they occur	• Telling about forms of identification & when needed • Comparing the governments of different countries • Describing how people in a community "exercise their 1st Amendment rights" • Brainstorming ideas for a new amendment to the Constitution • Describing U.S. holidays you celebrate • Describing holidays celebrated in different countries	0.1.2, 0.1.3, 2.7.1, 5.1.6, 5.2.1, 5.2.2, 5.5.2, 5.5.3, 5.5.4	*Beg. Low:* 40 *Beg. High:* 40, 42	*Literacy LCPs:* 01, 07, 15 *LCP A:* 12 *LCP B:* 26, 29 *LCP C:* 43, 46

Welcome to the second edition of the WORD BY WORD BASIC Picture Dictionary! This text presents more than 2,500 vocabulary words through vibrant illustrations and simple accessible lesson pages with large type that are designed for clarity and ease-of-use with learners at low-beginning and literacy levels. Our goal is to prepare students for success using English in everyday life, in the community, in school, and at work. We are delighted to now include as bonus material the WordSongs Music CD, offering students entertaining musical practice to extend learning outside the classroom.

WORD BY WORD BASIC is an abridged version of the "full" *Word by Word* Picture Dictionary. It organizes the vocabulary into 16 thematic units, providing a careful research-based sequence of lessons that integrates students' development of grammar and vocabulary skills through topics that begin with the immediate world of the student and progress to the world at large. Early lessons on the family, the home, and daily activities lead to lessons on the community, school, workplace, shopping, recreation, and other topics. The text offers extensive coverage of important lifeskill competencies and the vocabulary of school subjects and extracurricular activities, and it is designed to meet the objectives of current national, state, and local standards-based curricula you can find in the Scope & Sequence on the previous pages.

Since each lesson in *Word by Word Basic* is self-contained, it can be used either sequentially or in any desired order. For users' convenience, the lessons are listed in two ways: sequentially in the Table of Contents, and alphabetically in the Thematic Index. These resources, combined with the Glossary in the appendix, allow students and teachers to quickly and easily locate all words and topics in the Picture Dictionary.

The *Word by Word Basic* Picture Dictionary is the centerpiece of the complete *Word by Word Basic* Vocabulary Development Program, which offers a wide selection of print and media support materials for instruction at all levels.

A unique choice of workbooks offers flexible options to meet students' needs. A Vocabulary Workbook features motivating vocabulary, grammar, and listening practice. A standards-based Lifeskills Workbook provides competency-based activities and reading tied to national, state, and local curriculum frameworks. A Literacy Workbook offers fundamental practice with the alphabet and basic reading and writing skills for pre-Beginners.

The Teacher's Guide and Lesson Planner with CD-ROM includes lesson-planning suggestions, community tasks, Internet weblinks, and reproducible masters to save teachers hours of lesson preparation time. A Handbook of Vocabulary Teaching Strategies is included in the Teacher's Guide. The CD-ROM contains a complete Activity Bank of reproducible grammar and vocabulary worksheets for each unit and innovative level-specific lesson-planning forms that teachers can fill in and print out for quick and easy lesson preparation.

The Music CD included with this student book contains vocal versions of all the WordSongs. The separate Audio Program includes all words and conversations in the student book for interactive practice, plus both vocal and sing-along versions of all the WordSongs for entertaining classroom practice through music.

Additional ancillary materials include Color Transparencies, Vocabulary Game Cards, and a Testing Program. Bilingual Editions are also available.

Teaching Strategies

Word by Word Basic presents vocabulary words in context. Model conversations depict situations in which people use the words in meaningful communication. These models become the basis for students to engage in dynamic, interactive practice. In addition, writing and discussion questions in each lesson encourage students to relate the vocabulary and themes to their own lives as they share experiences, thoughts, opinions, and information about themselves, their cultures, and their countries. In this way, students get to know each other "word by word."

In using *Word by Word Basic*, we encourage you to develop approaches and strategies that are compatible with your own teaching style and the needs and abilities of your students. You may find it helpful to incorporate some of the following techniques for presenting and practicing the vocabulary in each lesson.

1. **Preview the Vocabulary:** Activate students' prior knowledge of the vocabulary by brainstorming with students the words in the lesson they already know and writing them on the board, or by having students look at the transparency or the illustration in *Word by Word Basic* and identify the words they are familiar with.

2. **Present the Vocabulary:** Using the transparency or the illustration in the Picture Dictionary, point to the picture of each word, say the word, and have the class repeat it chorally and individually. (You can also play the word list on the Audio Program.) Check students' understanding and pronunciation of the vocabulary.

3. **Vocabulary Practice:** Have students practice the vocabulary as a class, in pairs, or in small groups. Say or write a word, and have students point to the item or tell the number. Or, point to an item or give the number, and have students say the word.

4. **Model Conversation Practice:** Some lessons have model conversations that use the first word in the vocabulary list. Other models are in the form of skeletal dialogs, in which vocabulary words can be inserted. (In many skeletal dialogs, bracketed numbers indicate which words can be used for practicing the conversation. If no bracketed numbers appear, all the words in the lesson can be used.)

The following steps are recommended for Model Conversation Practice:

a. Preview: Have students look at the model illustration and discuss who they think the speakers are and where the conversation takes place.

b. The teacher presents the model or plays the audio one or more times and checks students' understanding of the situation and the vocabulary.

c. Students repeat each line of the conversation chorally and individually.

d. Students practice the model in pairs.

e. A pair of students presents a conversation based on the model, but using a different word from the vocabulary list.

f. In pairs, students practice several conversations based on the model, using different words on the page.

g. Pairs present their conversations to the class.

5. **Additional Conversation Practice:** Many lessons provide two additional skeletal dialogs for further conversation practice with the vocabulary. (These can be found in the yellow-shaded area at the bottom of the page.) Have students practice and present these conversations using any words they wish. Before they practice the additional conversations, you may want to have students listen to the sample additional conversations on the Audio Program.

6. **Spelling Practice:** Have students practice spelling the words as a class, in pairs, or in small groups. Say a word, and have students spell it aloud or write it. Or, using the transparency, point to an item and have students write the word.

7. **Themes for Discussion, Composition, Journals, and Portfolios:** Each lesson of *Word by Word Basic* provides one or more questions for discussion and composition. (These can be found in a blue-shaded area at the bottom of the page.) Have students respond to the questions as a class, in pairs, or in small groups. Or, have students write their responses at home, share their written work with other students, and discuss as a class, in pairs, or in small groups. As an alternative for students at literacy and pre-beginning levels, you can use a language experience approach by having students say their responses while you or a teaching assistant or a volunteer writes them down. Students can then practice decoding what they have "written" and then read their responses aloud to another student.

Students may enjoy keeping a journal of their written work. If time permits, you may want to write a response in each student's journal, sharing your own opinions and experiences as well as reacting to what the student has written. If you are keeping portfolios of students' work, these compositions serve as excellent examples of students' progress in learning English.

8. **Communication Activities:** The *Word by Word Basic* Teacher's Guide and Lesson Planner with CD-ROM provides a wealth of games, tasks, brainstorming, discussion, movement, drawing, miming, role-playing, and other activities designed to take advantage of students' different learning styles and particular abilities and strengths. For each lesson, choose one or more of these activities to reinforce students' vocabulary learning in a way that is stimulating, creative, and enjoyable.

WORD BY WORD BASIC aims to offer students a communicative, meaningful, and lively way of practicing English vocabulary. In conveying to you the substance of our program, we hope that we have also conveyed the spirit: that learning vocabulary can be genuinely interactive . . . relevant to our students' lives . . . responsive to students' differing strengths and learning styles . . . and fun!

Steven J. Molinsky
Bill Bliss

Registration Form

Name   Gloria   P.   Sanchez

            First   Middle Initial   Last

Address   95   Garden Street   3G

            Number   Street   Apartment Number

            Los Angeles   CA   90036

            City   State   Zip Code

Telephone   323-524-3278   Cell Phone   323-695-1864

E-Mail Address   gloria97@ail.com   SSN   227-93-6185   Sex M__ F **X**

Date of Birth   5/12/88   Place of Birth   Centerville, Texas

1 name
2 first name
3 middle initial
4 last name / family name
5 address
6 street number
7 street
8 apartment number
9 city
10 state
11 zip code

12 area code
13 telephone number /
   phone number
14 cell phone number
15 e-mail address
16 social security number
17 sex
18 date of birth
19 place of birth

A. What's your **name**?
B. Gloria P. Sanchez.

A. What's your _____?
B. ....
A. Did you say ....?
B. Yes. That's right.

A. What's your last name?
B. ....
A. How do you spell that?
B. ....

Tell about yourself:
   My name is ....
   My address is ....
   My telephone number is ....

Now interview a friend:
   What's your name?
   What's your address?
   What's your telephone number?

1 husband
2 wife

parents
3 father
4 mother

children
5 daughter
6 son
7 baby

siblings
8 sister
9 brother

grandparents
10 grandmother
11 grandfather

grandchildren
12 granddaughter
13 grandson

A. Who is he?
B. He's my **husband**.
A. What's his name?
B. His name is *Jack*.

A. Who is she?
B. She's my **wife**.
A. What's her name?
B. Her name is *Nancy*.

A. I'd like to introduce my _____.
B. Nice to meet you.
C. Nice to meet you, too.

A. What's your _____'s name?
B. His/Her name is ....

Who are the people in your family?
What are their names?

Tell about photos of family members.

Helen

Walter

Jack

Nancy

Frank

Linda

Jennifer

Timmy

Alan

1 uncle
2 aunt
3 niece

4 nephew
5 cousin

6 mother-in-law
7 father-in-law

8 son-in-law
9 daughter-in-law
10 brother-in-law
11 sister-in-law

① Jack is Alan's ___.
② Nancy is Alan's ___.
③ Jennifer is Frank and Linda's ___.
④ Timmy is Frank and Linda's ___.
⑤ Alan is Jennifer and Timmy's ___.

⑥ Helen is Jack's ___.
⑦ Walter is Jack's ___.
⑧ Jack is Helen and Walter's ___.
⑨ Linda is Helen and Walter's ___.
⑩ Frank is Jack's ___.
⑪ Linda is Jack's ___.

A. Who is he/she?
B. He's/She's my _____.
A. What's his/her name?
B. His/Her name is _____.

A. Let me introduce my _____.
B. I'm glad to meet you.
C. Nice meeting you, too.

Tell about your relatives:
   What are their names?
   Where do they live?

Draw your family tree and tell about it.

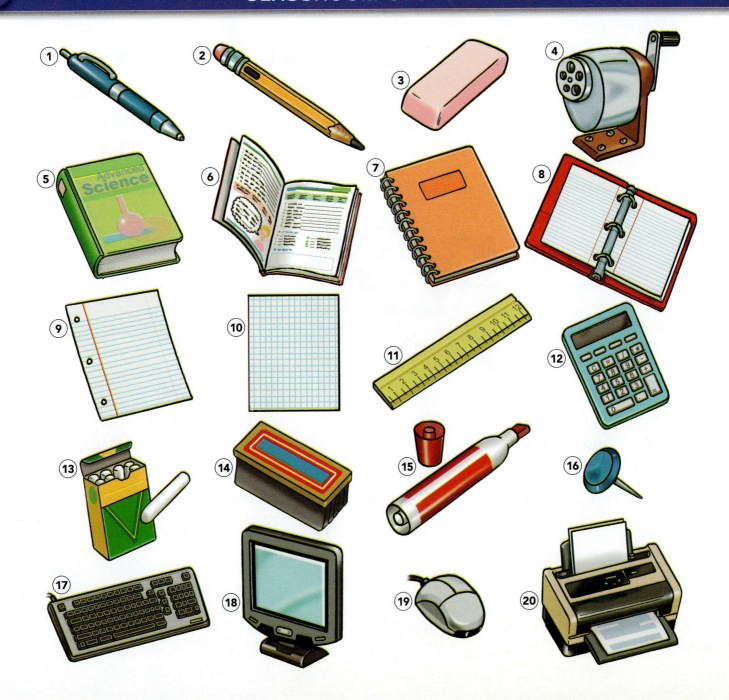

1 pen
2 pencil
3 eraser
4 pencil sharpener
5 book/textbook
6 workbook
7 spiral notebook
8 binder/notebook

9 notebook paper
10 graph paper
11 ruler
12 calculator
13 chalk
14 eraser
15 marker
16 thumbtack

17 keyboard
18 monitor
19 mouse
20 printer

[1, 2, 4–8, 11, 12, 15–20]
A. What do you call this in English?
B. It's a **pen**.*

* With 9, 10, 13 use: It's _____ .

[3, 14]
A. What do you call this in English?
B. It's an **eraser**.

A. Where's the _____ ?
B. Over there.

[1–3, 5–12]
A. Is this your _____ ?
B. Yes, it is.

Point to objects and people in your classroom and say the words.

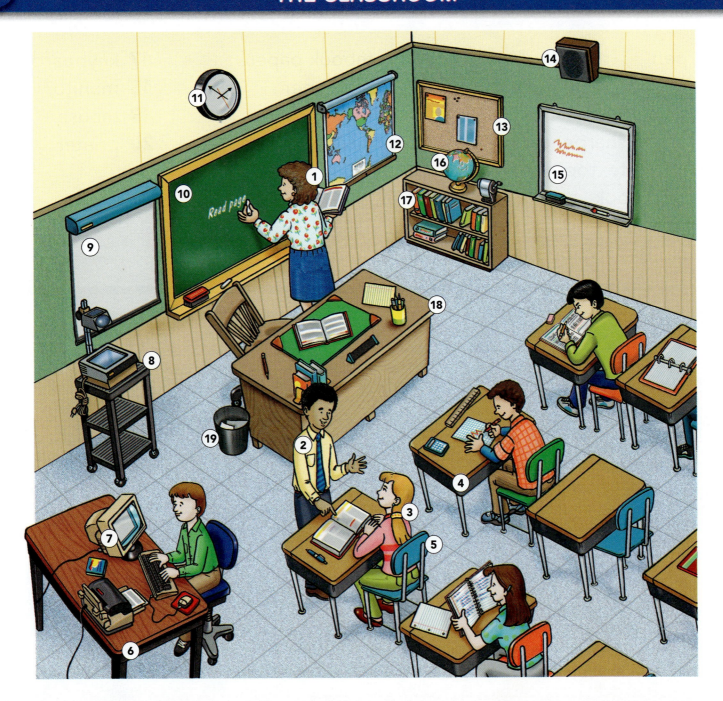

1 teacher
2 teacher's aide
3 student
4 desk
5 seat/chair
6 table
7 computer

8 overhead projector
9 screen
10 board/chalkboard
11 clock
12 map
13 bulletin board

14 P.A. system/loudspeaker
15 whiteboard
16 globe
17 bookcase/bookshelf
18 teacher's desk
19 wastebasket

Practice these conversations with the words on pages 8–11.

A. Where's the **teacher**?
B. The **teacher** is *next to* the **board**.

A. Where's the **globe**?
B. The **globe** is *on* the **bookcase**.

A. Is there a/an _____ in your classroom?*
B. Yes. There's a/an _____ next to/on the _____.

A. Is there a/an _____ in your classroom?*
B. No, there isn't.

Describe your classroom. (There's a/an ....)

* *With 9, 10, 13 on page 9 use:* Is there _____ in your classroom?

1 Say your name.
2 Repeat your name.
3 Spell your name.
4 Print your name.
5 Sign your name.

11 Open your book.
12 Read page ten.
13 Study page ten.
14 Close your book.
15 Put away your book.

6 Stand up.
7 Go to the board.
8 Write on the board.
9 Erase the board.
10 Sit down. / Take your seat.

16 Raise your hand.
17 Ask a question.
18 Listen to the question.
19 Answer the question.
20 Listen to the answer.

You're the teacher.
Give instructions to your students.

1 Do your homework.
2 Bring in your homework.
3 Go over the answers.
4 Correct your mistakes.
5 Hand in your homework.

6 Share a book.
7 Discuss the question.
8 Help each other.
9 Work together.
10 Share with the class.

11 Look in the dictionary.
12 Look up a word.
13 Pronounce the word.
14 Read the definition.
15 Copy the word.

16 Work alone./Do your own work.
17 Work with a partner.
18 Break up into small groups.
19 Work in a group.
20 Work as a class.

You're the teacher.
Give instructions to your students.

1 Lower the shades.
2 Turn off the lights.
3 Look at the screen.
4 Take notes.
5 Turn on the lights.

6 Take out a piece of paper.
7 Pass out the tests.
8 Answer the questions.
9 Check your answers.
10 Collect the tests.

11 Choose the correct answer.
12 Circle the correct answer.
13 Fill in the blank.
14 Mark the answer sheet. / Bubble the answer.
15 Match the words.

16 Underline the word.
17 Cross out the word.
18 Unscramble the word.
19 Put the words in order.
20 Write on a separate sheet of paper.

You're the teacher.
Give instructions to your students.

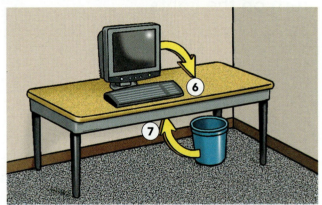

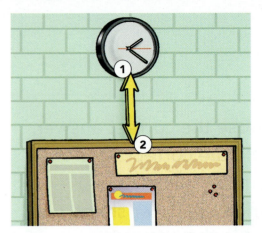

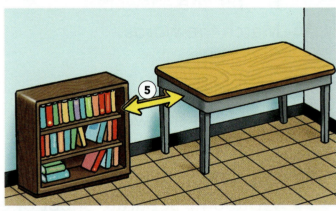

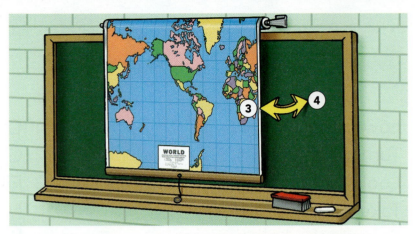

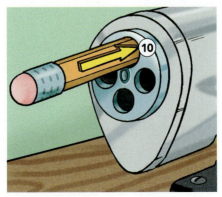

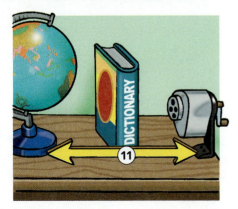

1 above

2 below

3 in front of

4 behind

5 next to

6 on

7 under

8 to the left of

9 to the right of

10 in

11 between

[1–10]

A. Where's the *clock*?

B. The *clock* is **above** the *bulletin board*.

[11]

A. Where's the *dictionary*?

B. The *dictionary* is **between** the *globe* and the *pencil sharpener*.

Tell about the classroom on page 10. Use the prepositions in this lesson.

Tell about your classroom.

A office
B principal's office
C nurse's office
D guidance office
E classroom
F hallway
  a locker
G science lab
H gym
  a locker room
I track
  a bleachers

J field
K auditorium
L cafeteria
M library

1 clerk / (school) secretary
2 principal
3 school nurse
4 guidance counselor
5 teacher
6 assistant principal /
   vice-principal

7 security officer
8 science teacher
9 P.E. teacher
10 coach
11 custodian
12 cafeteria worker
13 lunchroom monitor
14 school librarian

A. Where are you going?
B. I'm going to the ___[A–D, G–M]___ .
A. Do you have a hall pass?
B. Yes. Here it is.

A. Where's the ___[1–14]___ ?
B. He's } in the ___[A–M]___ .
   She's

Describe the school where you study English. Tell about the rooms, offices, and people.

Tell about differences between the school in this lesson and schools in your country.

1 get up
2 take a shower
3 brush *my** teeth
4 shave
5 get dressed
6 wash *my** face
7 put on makeup
8 brush *my** hair
9 comb *my** hair
10 make the bed

* my, his, her, our, your, their

11 get undressed
12 take a bath
13 go to bed
14 sleep
15 make breakfast
16 make lunch
17 cook / make dinner
18 eat / have breakfast
19 eat / have lunch
20 eat / have dinner

A. What do you do every day?
B. I **get up**, I **take a shower**, and I **brush my teeth**.

A. What does he do every day?
B. He _____s, he _____s,
   and he _____s.

A. What does she do every day?
B. She _____s, she _____s,
   and she_____s.

What do you do every day? Make a list.

Interview some friends and tell about their everyday activities.

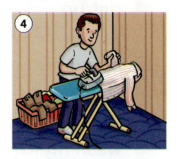

1 clean the apartment/clean the house
2 wash the dishes
3 do the laundry
4 iron
5 feed the baby
6 feed the cat
7 walk the dog
8 study

9 go to work
10 go to school
11 drive to work
12 take the bus to school
13 work
14 leave work
15 go to the store
16 come home

A. Hello. What are you doing?
B. I'm **clean**ing the **apartment**.

A. Hello, ... This is ....
   What are you doing?
B. I'm _____ing. How about you?
A. I'm _____ing.

A. Are you going to _____ soon?
B. Yes. I'm going to _____ in a
   little while.

What are you going to do tomorrow?
Make a list of everything you are
going to do.

1 watch TV
2 listen to the radio
3 listen to music
4 read a book
5 read the newspaper
6 play
7 play cards
8 play basketball

9 play the guitar
10 practice the piano
11 exercise
12 swim
13 plant flowers
14 use the computer
15 write a letter
16 relax

A. Hi. What are you doing?
B. I'm **watch**ing **TV**.

A. Hi, ... Are you _____ing?
B. No, I'm not. I'm _____ing.

A. What's your (husband / wife / son / daughter / . . .) doing?
B. He's / She's _____ing.

What leisure activities do you like to do?

What do your family members and friends like to do?

Greeting People

Leave Taking

1 Hello. / Hi.

2 Good morning.

3 Good afternoon.

4 Good evening.

5 How are you? / How are you doing?

6 Fine. / Fine, thanks. / Okay.

7 What's new? / What's new with you?

8 Not much. / Not too much.

9 Good-bye. / Bye.

10 Good night.

11 See you later. / See you soon.

Practice conversations with other students.
Use all the expressions in this lesson.

Introducing Yourself and Others

Getting Someone's Attention

Expressing Gratitude

Saying You Don't Understand

Calling Someone on the Telephone

1 Hello. My name is .... / Hi. I'm ....

2 Nice to meet you.

3 Nice to meet you, too.

4 I'd like to introduce .... / This is ....

5 Excuse me.

6 May I ask a question?

7 Thank you. / Thanks.

8 You're welcome.

9 I don't understand. / Sorry. I don't understand.

10 Can you please repeat that? / Can you please say that again?

11 Hello. This is .... May I please speak to ....?

12 Yes. Hold on a moment.

13 I'm sorry. .... isn't here right now.

Practice conversations with other students.
Use all the expressions in this lesson.

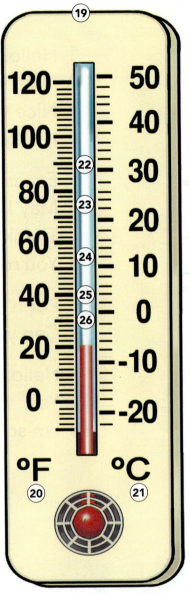

Weather

1 sunny
2 cloudy
3 clear
4 hazy
5 foggy
6 smoggy

7 windy
8 humid / muggy
9 raining
10 drizzling
11 snowing
12 hailing

13 sleeting
14 lightning
15 thunderstorm
16 snowstorm
17 dust storm
18 heat wave

Temperature

19 thermometer
20 Fahrenheit
21 Centigrade / Celsius
22 hot
23 warm
24 cool
25 cold
26 freezing

[1–13]
A. What's the weather like?
B. It's _____.

[14–18]
A. What's the weather forecast?
B. There's going to be { [14] .
a [15–18] .

[20–26]
A. How's the weather?
B. It's [22–26] .
A. What's the temperature?
B. It's . . . degrees [20–21] .

What's the weather like today? What's the temperature?

What's the weather forecast for tomorrow?

0	zero	11	eleven	21	twenty-one	101	one hundred (and) one
1	one	12	twelve	22	twenty-two	102	one hundred (and) two
2	two	13	thirteen	30	thirty	1,000	one thousand
3	three	14	fourteen	40	forty	10,000	ten thousand
4	four	15	fifteen	50	fifty	100,000	one hundred thousand
5	five	16	sixteen	60	sixty	1,000,000	one million
6	six	17	seventeen	70	seventy	1,000,000,000	one billion
7	seven	18	eighteen	80	eighty		
8	eight	19	nineteen	90	ninety		
9	nine	20	twenty	100	one hundred		
10	ten						

A. How old are you?

B. I'm _____ years old.

A. How many people are there in your family?

B. _____.

How many students are there in your class?

How many people are there in your country?

1st	first	11th	eleventh	21st	twenty-first	101st	one hundred (and) first
2nd	second	12th	twelfth	22nd	twenty-second	102nd	one hundred (and) second
3rd	third	13th	thirteenth	30th	thirtieth	1,000th	one thousandth
4th	fourth	14th	fourteenth	40th	fortieth	10,000th	ten thousandth
5th	fifth	15th	fifteenth	50th	fiftieth	100,000th	one hundred thousandth
6th	sixth	16th	sixteenth	60th	sixtieth	1,000,000th	one millionth
7th	seventh	17th	seventeenth	70th	seventieth	1,000,000,000th	one billionth
8th	eighth	18th	eighteenth	80th	eightieth		
9th	ninth	19th	nineteenth	90th	ninetieth		
10th	tenth	20th	twentieth	100th	one hundredth		

A. What floor do you live on?
B. I live on the _____ floor.

A. Is this your first trip to our country?
B. No. It's my _____ trip.

What were the names of your teachers in elementary school?
(My *first*-grade teacher was Ms./Mrs./Mr. . . .)

two o'clock

two fifteen /
a quarter after *two*

two thirty /
half past *two*

two forty-five /
a quarter to *three*

two oh five

two twenty /
twenty after *two*

two forty /
twenty to *three*

two fifty-five /
five to *three*

A. What time is it?
B. It's _____ .

A. What time does the movie begin?
B. At _____ .

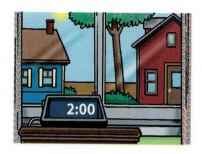

two A.M.

two P.M.

noon /
twelve noon

midnight /
twelve midnight

A. When does the train leave?
B. At _____.

A. What time will we arrive?
B. At _____.

Tell about your daily schedule:
  What do you do? When?
  (I get up at _____. I ....)

Tell about the use of time in different cultures or countries you know:
  Do people arrive on time for work? appointments? parties?
  Do trains and buses operate exactly on schedule?
  Do movies and sports events begin on time?
  Do workplaces use time clocks or timesheets to record employees' work hours?

1 2 3 4 5  6

Name	Value	Written as:	
1 penny	one cent	1¢	$ .01
2 nickel	five cents	5¢	$ .05
3 dime	ten cents	10¢	$ .10
4 quarter	twenty-five cents	25¢	$ .25
5 half dollar	fifty cents	50¢	$ .50
6 silver dollar	one dollar		$1.00

A. How much is a **penny** worth?

B. A **penny** is worth **one cent**.

A. *Soda* costs *ninety-five cents.*
   Do you have enough change?

B. Yes. I have a/two/three ____(s) and . . . .

Name	We sometimes say:	Value	Written as:
1 (one-) dollar bill	a one	one dollar	$ 1.00
2 five-dollar bill	a five	five dollars	$ 5.00
3 ten-dollar bill	a ten	ten dollars	$ 10.00
4 twenty-dollar bill	a twenty	twenty dollars	$ 20.00
5 fifty-dollar bill	a fifty	fifty dollars	$ 50.00
6 (one-) hundred dollar bill	a hundred	one hundred dollars	$100.00

A. Do you have any cash?
B. Yes. I have a **twenty-dollar bill**.

A. Can you change a **five-dollar bill**?
B. Yes. I have *five one-dollar bills*.

Written as:	We say:
$1.30	a dollar and thirty cents
	a dollar thirty
$2.50	two dollars and fifty cents
	two fifty
$56.49	fifty-six dollars and forty-nine cents
	fifty-six forty-nine

Tell about some things you usually buy.
What do they cost?

Name and describe the coins and currency in your country.
What are they worth in U.S. dollars?

① 2012
② JANUARY

SUN ⑥	MON ⑦	TUE ⑧	WED ⑨	THU ⑩	FRI ⑪	SAT ⑫
1	2	3	4	5	6	7
8	9	10	11	12	13	14
15	16	17	18	19	20	21
22	23	24	25	26	27	28
29	30	31				

③
④
⑤

⑬ JAN ⑭ FEB ⑮ MAR
⑯ APR ⑰ MAY ⑱ JUN
⑲ JUL ⑳ AUG ㉑ SEP
㉒ OCT ㉓ NOV ㉔ DEC

2012 JANUARY

㉕ 1/3/12
JAN 3 2012

㉖

HAPPY 25th
㉗

㉘ APPOINTMENT
Charles Wong, M.D.
Date: February 21
Time: 3:00 PM

Days of the Week

1 year
2 month
3 week
4 day
5 weekend

6 Sunday
7 Monday
8 Tuesday
9 Wednesday
10 Thursday
11 Friday
12 Saturday

Months of the Year

13 January
14 February
15 March
16 April
17 May
18 June

19 July
20 August
21 September
22 October
23 November
24 December

25 January 3, 2012
   January third, two
      thousand twelve
26 birthday
27 anniversary
28 appointment

A. What year is it?
B. It's _____.

[13–24]
A. What month is it?
B. It's _____.

[6–12]
A. What day is it?
B. It's _____.

A. What's today's date?
B. It's _____.

[26–28]
A. When is your _____?
B. It's on _____.

Which days of the week do you
go to work/school?
(I go to work/school on _____.)

What is your date of birth?
(I was born on ...*month day, year*....)

What's your favorite day of the week? Why?

What's your favorite month of the year?
Why?

1 yesterday
2 today
3 tomorrow

4 morning
5 afternoon
6 evening
7 night

8 yesterday morning
9 yesterday afternoon
10 yesterday evening
11 last night

12 this morning
13 this afternoon
14 this evening
15 tonight

16 tomorrow morning
17 tomorrow afternoon
18 tomorrow evening
19 tomorrow night

20 last week
21 this week
22 next week

23 once a week
24 twice a week
25 three times a week
26 every day

Seasons
27 spring
28 summer
29 fall/autumn
30 winter

What did you do yesterday morning/afternoon/evening?

What did you do last night?

What are you going to do tomorrow morning/afternoon/evening/night?

What did you do last week?

What are your plans for next week?

How many times a week do you have English class?/go to the supermarket?/exercise?

What's your favorite season? Why?

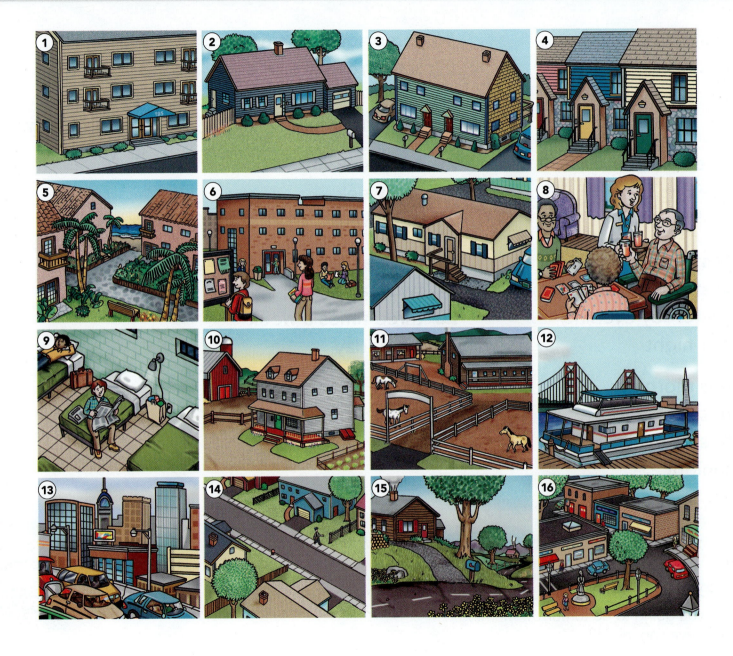

1 apartment building
2 house
3 duplex/two-family house
4 townhouse/townhome
5 condominium/condo
6 dormitory/dorm
7 mobile home
8 nursing home

9 shelter
10 farm
11 ranch
12 houseboat
13 the city
14 the suburbs
15 the country
16 a town/village

A. Where do you live?
B. I live { in a/an ___[1–9]___.
           on a ___[10–12]___.
           in ___[13–16]___.

[1–12]
A. Town Taxi Company.
B. Hello. Please send a taxi to
   ....(address).....
A. Is that a house or an
   apartment building?
B. It's a/an _____.
A. All right. We'll be there
   right away.

[1–12]
A. This is the Emergency Operator.
B. Please send an ambulance to
   ....(address).....
A. Is that a private home?
B. It's a/an _____.
A. What's your name and telephone number?
B. ....

Tell about people you know and
where they live.

Discuss:
   Who lives in dormitories?
   Who lives in nursing homes?
   Who lives in shelters?
   Why?

1 bookcase
2 picture / photograph
3 painting
4 mantel
5 fireplace
6 fireplace screen
7 DVD player
8 television / TV
9 VCR / video cassette recorder

10 wall
11 ceiling
12 drapes
13 window
14 loveseat
15 wall unit
16 speaker
17 stereo system
18 magazine holder
19 pillow

20 sofa / couch
21 plant
22 coffee table
23 rug
24 lamp
25 lampshade
26 end table
27 floor
28 floor lamp
29 armchair

A. Where are you?
B. I'm in the living room.
A. What are you doing?
B. I'm dusting* the **bookcase**.

*dusting / cleaning

A. You have a very nice living room!
B. Thank you.
A. Your _____ is / are beautiful!
B. Thank you for saying so.

A. Uh-oh! I just spilled coffee on your _____!
B. That's okay. Don't worry about it.

Tell about your living room.
(In my living room there's ....)

1 (dining room) table
2 (dining room) chair
3 buffet
4 tray
5 teapot
6 coffee pot
7 sugar bowl
8 creamer
9 pitcher
10 chandelier
11 china cabinet

12 china
13 salad bowl
14 serving bowl
15 serving dish
16 vase
17 candle
18 candlestick
19 platter
20 butter dish
21 salt shaker
22 pepper shaker

23 tablecloth
24 napkin
25 fork
26 plate
27 knife
28 spoon
29 bowl
30 mug
31 glass
32 cup
33 saucer

A. This **dining room table** is very nice.
B. Thank you. It was a gift from my *grandmother.**

*grandmother / grandfather / aunt / uncle / . . .

[In a store]
A. May I help you?
B. Yes, please. Do you have _____s?*
A. Yes. _____s* are right over there.
B. Thank you.

*With 12, use the singular.

[At home]
A. Where did you get this old _____?
B. At a yard sale. How do you like it?
A. It's VERY unusual!

Tell about your dining room.
(In my dining room there's
.............)

1 bed
2 headboard
3 pillow
4 pillowcase
5 sheet
6 blanket
7 electric blanket
8 bedspread

9 comforter/quilt
10 carpet
11 chest (of drawers)
12 blinds
13 curtains
14 lamp
15 alarm clock
16 clock radio

17 night table/nightstand
18 mirror
19 jewelry box
20 dresser/bureau
21 mattress
22 box spring
23 bed frame

A. Ooh! Look at that big bug!
B. Where?
A. It's on the **bed**!
B. I'LL get it.

[In a store]
A. Excuse me. I'm looking for
   a/an _____.*
B. We have some very nice _____s,
   and they're all on sale this week!
A. Oh, good!

* With 12 & 13, use: Excuse me. I'm looking for ____.

[In a bedroom]
A. Oh, no! I just lost my
   contact lens!
B. Where?
A. I think it's on the _____.
B. I'll help you look.

Tell about your bedroom.
(In my bedroom there's ....)

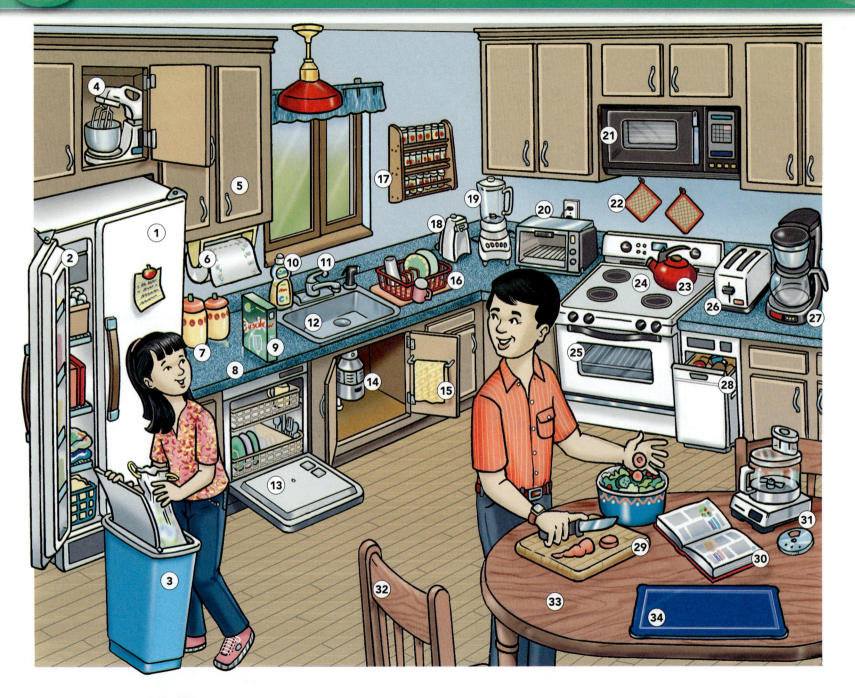

1 refrigerator
2 freezer
3 garbage pail
4 (electric) mixer
5 cabinet
6 paper towel holder
7 canister
8 counter
9 dishwasher detergent
10 dishwashing liquid
11 faucet
12 sink

13 dishwasher
14 (garbage) disposal
15 dish towel
16 dish rack
17 spice rack
18 (electric) can opener
19 blender
20 toaster oven
21 microwave
22 potholder
23 tea kettle

24 stove/range
25 oven
26 toaster
27 coffeemaker
28 trash compactor
29 cutting board
30 cookbook
31 food processor
32 kitchen chair
33 kitchen table
34 placemat

A. I think we need a new **refrigerator**.
B. I think you're right.

[In a store]
A. Excuse me. Are your _____s still on sale?
B. Yes, they are. They're twenty percent off.

[In a kitchen]
A. When did you get this/these new _____(s)?
B. I got it/them last week.

Tell about your kitchen. (In my kitchen there's ....)

1 teddy bear
2 baby monitor/intercom
3 chest (of drawers)
4 crib
5 mobile
6 changing table
7 stretch suit
8 diaper pail
9 night light
10 toy chest

11 stuffed animal
12 doll
13 swing
14 playpen
15 rattle
16 walker
17 cradle
18 stroller
19 baby carriage
20 car seat/safety seat

21 baby carrier
22 food warmer
23 booster seat
24 baby seat
25 high chair
26 portable crib
27 potty
28 baby frontpack
29 baby backpack

A. Thank you for the **teddy bear**. It's a very nice gift.
B. You're welcome.

A. That's a very nice _____.
   Where did you get it?
B. It was a gift from ....

A. Do you have everything you need
   before the baby comes?
B. Almost everything. We're still
   looking for a/an _____ and
   a/an _____.

Tell about your country:
   What things do people buy for a new baby?
   Does a new baby sleep in a separate room,
   as in the United States?

1 wastebasket
2 vanity
3 soap
4 soap dish
5 soap dispenser
6 sink
7 faucet
8 medicine cabinet
9 mirror
10 cup
11 toothbrush

12 electric toothbrush
13 hair dryer
14 shelf
15 hamper
16 fan
17 towel
18 towel rack
19 plunger
20 toilet brush
21 toilet paper
22 air freshener

23 toilet
24 toilet seat
25 shower
26 shower curtain
27 bathtub/tub
28 rubber mat
29 drain
30 sponge
31 bath mat
32 scale

A. Where's the **hair dryer**?
B. It's *on* the **vanity**.

A. Where's the **soap**?
B. It's *in* the **soap dish**.

A. Where's the **plunger**?
B. It's *next to* the **toilet brush**.

A. [Knock. Knock.] Did I leave my glasses in there?
B. Yes. They're *on* / *in* / *next to* the _____.

A. *Bobby*? You didn't clean up the bathroom! There's toothpaste on the _____, and there's powder all over the _____!
B. Sorry. I'll clean it up right away.

Tell about your bathroom.
(In my bathroom there's ....)

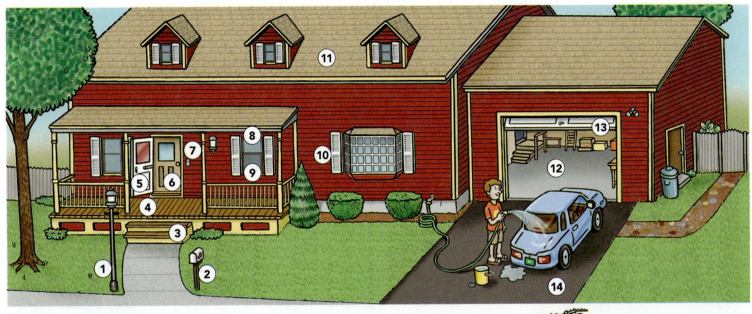

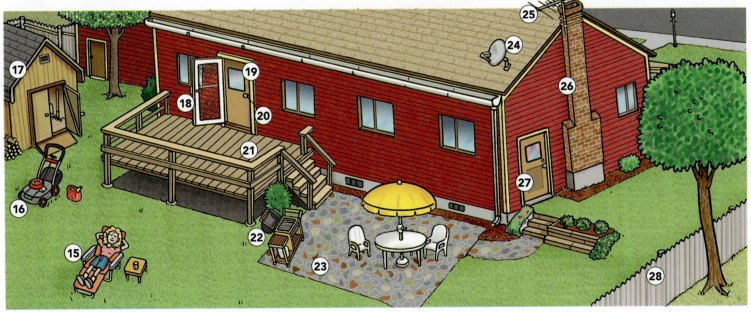

Front Yard

1 lamppost
2 mailbox
3 front steps
4 front porch
5 storm door
6 front door
7 doorbell

8 window
9 window screen
10 shutter
11 roof
12 garage
13 garage door
14 driveway

Backyard

15 lawn chair
16 lawnmower
17 tool shed
18 screen door
19 back door
20 door knob
21 deck

22 barbecue/grill
23 patio
24 satellite dish
25 TV antenna
26 chimney
27 side door
28 fence

A. When are you going to repair the **lamppost**?
B. I'm going to repair it next Saturday.

[On the telephone]
A. Harry's Home Repairs.
B. Hello. Do you fix _____s?
A. No, we don't.
B. Oh, okay. Thank you.

[At work on Monday morning]
A. What did you do this weekend?
B. Nothing much. I repaired my _____ and my _____.

Do you like to repair things?
What things can you repair yourself?
What things can't you repair? Who repairs them?

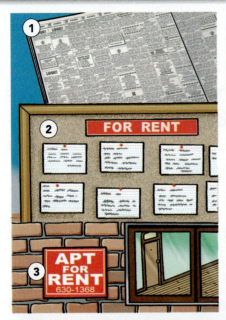

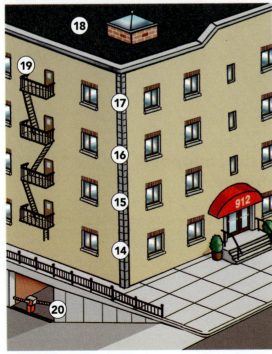

Looking for an Apartment

1 apartment ads/
classified ads
2 apartment listings
3 vacancy sign

Signing a Lease

4 tenant
5 landlord
6 lease
7 security deposit

Moving In

8 moving truck/
moving van
9 neighbor
10 building manager
11 doorman
12 key
13 lock
14 first floor
15 second floor
16 third floor
17 fourth floor

18 roof
19 fire escape
20 parking garage
21 balcony
22 courtyard
23 parking lot
24 parking space
25 swimming pool
26 whirlpool
27 trash bin
28 air conditioner

[19–28]
A. Is there a **fire escape**?
B. Yes, there is.

[14–17]
A. What floor is the
apartment on?
B. It's on the _____.

[20, 22–27]
A. Where's the _____?
B. It's in back of the building.

How do people look for apartments in your
city or town?

Tell about an apartment building you know:
   How many floors are there?
   Is there an elevator?
   Is there a parking lot or parking garage?
   How many apartments are there in the building?

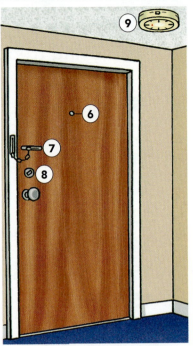

Lobby

1 intercom
2 buzzer
3 mailbox
4 elevator
5 stairway

Doorway

6 peephole
7 door chain
8 lock
9 smoke detector

Hallway

10 fire exit/emergency stairway
11 fire alarm
12 superintendent
13 sprinkler system
14 garbage chute/trash chute

Basement

15 storage room
16 storage locker
17 laundry room
18 security gate

[1, 4]
A. Is there an **intercom**?
B. Yes, there is.

[2, 3, 5–18]
A. Is there a **mailbox**?
B. Yes, there is.

[Renting an apartment]
A. Let me show you around.
B. Okay.
A. This is the _____, and here's the _____.
B. I see.

[On the telephone]
A. Mom and Dad? I found an apartment.
B. Good. Tell us about it.
A. It has a/an _____ and a/an _____.
B. That's nice. Does it have a/an _____?
A. Yes, it does.

Do you or someone you know live in an apartment building? Tell about it.

A plumber
1 The bathtub is leaking.
2 The sink is clogged.
3 The hot water heater isn't working.
4 The toilet is broken.

B roofer
5 The roof is leaking.

C (house) painter
6 The paint is peeling.
7 The wall is cracked.

D cable TV company
8 The cable TV isn't working.

E appliance repairperson
9 The stove isn't working.
10 The refrigerator is broken.

F exterminator/ pest control specialist
11 There are ____ in the kitchen.
a termites
b fleas
c ants
d bees
e cockroaches
f rats
g mice

A. What's the matter?
B. ___[1–11]___ .
A. I think we should call a/an ___[A–F]___ .

[1–11]
A. I'm having a problem in my apartment/house.
B. What's the problem?
A. _____ .

[A–F]
A. Can you recommend a good _____ ?
B. Yes. You should call ....

What do you do when you have these problems in your home? Do you fix things yourself, or do you call someone?

A locksmith
1 The lock is broken.

B electrician
2 The front light doesn't go on.
3 The doorbell doesn't ring.
4 The power is out in the living room.

C chimneysweep
5 The chimney is dirty.

D home repairperson/"handyman"
6 The tiles in the bathroom are loose.

E carpenter
7 The steps are broken.
8 The door doesn't open.

F heating and air conditioning service
9 The heating system is broken.
10 The air conditioning isn't working.

A. What's the matter?
B.   [1–10] .
A. I think we should call a/an   [A–F] .

[1–10]
A. I'm having a problem in my apartment/house.
B. What's the problem?
A. _____ .

[A–F]
A. Can you recommend a good _____?
B. Yes. You should call ....

What do you do when you have these problems in your home? Do you fix things yourself, or do you call someone?

A sweep the floor
B vacuum
C mop the floor
D wash the windows
E dust
F wax the floor
G polish the furniture
H clean the bathroom
I take out the garbage

1 broom
2 dustpan
3 whisk broom
4 carpet sweeper
5 vacuum (cleaner)
6 vacuum cleaner attachments
7 vacuum cleaner bag
8 hand vacuum

9 (dust) mop/ (dry) mop
10 (sponge) mop
11 (wet) mop
12 paper towels
13 window cleaner
14 ammonia
15 dust cloth
16 feather duster

17 floor wax
18 furniture polish
19 cleanser
20 scrub brush
21 sponge
22 bucket/pail
23 trash can/ garbage can
24 recycling bin

[A–I]
A. What are you doing?
B. I'm **sweep**ing **the floor**.

[1–24]
A. I can't find the **broom**.
B. Look over there!

[1–12, 15, 16, 20–24]
A. Excuse me. Do you sell _____(s)?
B. Yes. They're at the back of the store.
A. Thanks.

[13, 14, 17–19]
A. Excuse me. Do you sell _____?
B. Yes. It's at the back of the store.
A. Thanks.

What household cleaning chores do people do in your home? What things do they use?

1 hammer
2 saw
3 screwdriver
4 wrench
5 monkey wrench
6 vise
7 pliers
8 toolbox
9 electric drill
10 nail

11 washer
12 nut
13 screw
14 bolt
15 shovel
16 wheelbarrow
17 hose
18 rake
19 yardstick
20 flashlight

21 ladder
22 fly swatter
23 plunger
24 mousetrap
25 bug spray/insect spray
26 batteries
27 lightbulbs/bulbs
28 paint
29 paintbrush/brush
30 paint roller

A. I can't find the **hammer**!
B. Look in the utility cabinet.
A. Okay. Thanks.

* With 10–14, use: I can't find any _____s.

[1–9, 15–25, 29, 30]
A. Can I borrow your _____?
B. Sure.
A. Thanks.

[10–14, 26, 27]
A. Can I borrow some _____(s)?
B. Sure.
A. Thanks.

What tools and home supplies do you have? How and when do you use them?

1 bakery
2 bank
3 barber shop
4 book store

5 bus station
6 child-care center/day-care center
7 cleaners
8 clinic

9 clothing store
10 coffee shop
11 computer store
12 convenience store

A. Where are you going?
B. I'm going to the **bakery**.

A. Are you going to the _____?
B. No. I'm going to the _____.

A. Where did you go?
B. I went to the _____.

Which of these places are in your neighborhood?
(In my neighborhood there's a/an ....)

1 department store
2 discount store
3 donut shop
4 drug store/pharmacy

5 electronics store
6 eye-care center/optician
7 fast-food restaurant
8 flower shop/florist

9 furniture store
10 gas station/service station
11 grocery store
12 hair salon

A. Hi! How are you today?
B. Fine. Where are you going?
A. To the **department store**. How about you?
B. I'm going to the **discount store**.

A. I'm going to the _____.
B. See you later.
A. Bye.

A. Did you go to the _____ today?
B. No. I went to the _____.

Which of these places are in your neighborhood?
(In my neighborhood there's a/an ....)

1 hardware store
2 health club
3 hospital
4 hotel

5 ice cream shop
6 laundromat
7 library
8 maternity shop

9 motel
10 movie theater
11 music store
12 nail salon

A. Where's the **hardware store**?
B. It's right over there.

A. Excuse me. Where's
   the _____?
B. It's around the corner.
A. Thank you.

A. Excuse me. Is this the way
   to the _____?
B. Yes, it is.
A. Thanks.

Which of these places are in your neighborhood?
(In my neighborhood there's a/an ....)

1 park
2 pet shop
3 pizza shop
4 post office

5 restaurant
6 school
7 shoe store
8 (shopping) mall

9 supermarket
10 toy store
11 train station
12 video store

A. Is there a **park** nearby?
B. Yes. There's a **park** around the corner.

A. Excuse me. Is there a _____ near here?
B. Yes, there is. There's a _____ right over there.
A. Thank you.

A. Oh, no! I can't find my wallet/purse!
B. Did you leave it at the _____?
A. Maybe I did.

Which of these places are in your neighborhood?
(In my neighborhood there's a/an ....)

1 courthouse
2 taxi/cab
3 taxi stand
4 taxi driver/cab driver
5 fire hydrant
6 trash container
7 city hall

8 fire alarm box
9 mailbox
10 sewer
11 police station
12 jail
13 sidewalk
14 street

15 street light
16 parking lot
17 meter maid
18 parking meter
19 garbage truck
20 subway
21 subway station

A. Where's the _____?
B. On/In/Next to/Between/Across from/
   In front of/Behind/Under/Over the _____.

[1, 11, 12]
A. Excuse me. Where's the _____?
B. It's around the corner.

[3, 6, 8, 9, 16, 21]
A. Excuse me. Is there a _____ nearby?
B. Yes. There's a _____ down the street.

Which of these people, places, and things are in your neighborhood?

1 newsstand
2 traffic light
3 intersection
4 police officer
5 crosswalk
6 pedestrian
7 ice cream truck

8 curb
9 parking garage
10 fire station
11 bus stop
12 bus
13 bus driver
14 office building

15 public telephone
16 street sign
17 manhole
18 motorcycle
19 street vendor
20 drive-through window

A. Where's the _____?
B. On/In/Next to/Between/Across from/
   In front of/Behind/Under/Over the _____.

[4, 13, 19]
A. What do you do?
B. I'm a _____.

[1, 5, 7, 9–11, 14, 15]
A. Excuse me. Is there a/an _____ near here?
B. Yes. There's a/an _____ up the street.

Go to an intersection in your
city or town. What do you see?
Make a list. Then tell about it.
(Use the words on pages 80–83.)

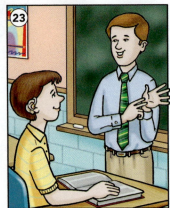

1 **child–children**
2 baby/infant
3 toddler
4 boy
5 girl
6 teenager

7 **adult**
8 man–men
9 woman–women
10 senior citizen

age
11 young
12 middle-aged
13 old

height
14 tall
15 average height
16 short

weight
17 heavy
18 average weight
19 thin/slim

20 pregnant

21 physically challenged
22 vision impaired
23 hearing impaired

A. Tell me about *your brother.*
B. He's *a tall heavy boy.*

A. Tell me about *your sister.*
B. She's *a short thin girl.*

A. Can you describe the person?
B. I think so.
A. What's *his* age?
B. *He's* ___[11–13]___ .
A. What's *his* height?
B. *He's* ___[14–16]___ .
A. What's *his* weight?
B. *He's* ___[17–19]___ .

Tell about yourself.   Tell about people in your family.

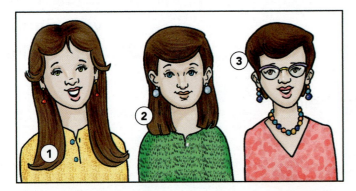

Describing Hair

1 long
2 shoulder length
3 short

4 straight
5 wavy
6 curly

7 black
8 brown
9 blond
10 red
11 gray

12 bald
13 beard
14 mustache

A. What does *your new boss* look like?
B. *She* has *long straight black* hair.

A. What does *your grandfather* look like?
B. *He* has *short curly gray* hair.

A. Can you describe *his* hair?
B. *He's bald*, and *he* has a *mustache*.

Tell about yourself.

Tell about people in your family.

Tell about your favorite actor or actress or other famous person.

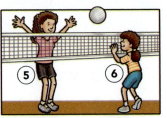

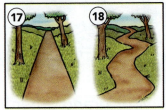

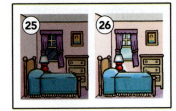

1–2	new – old		19–20	straight – curly
3–4	young – old		21–22	wide – narrow
5–6	tall – short		23–24	thick – thin
7–8	long – short		25–26	dark – light
9–10	large/big – small/little		27–28	high – low
11–12	fast – slow		29–30	loose – tight
13–14	heavy/fat – thin/skinny		31–32	good – bad
15–16	heavy – light		33–34	hot – cold
17–18	straight – crooked		35–36	neat – messy

[1–2]
A. Is your car **new**?
B. No. It's **old**.

1–2 Is your car _____?
3–4 Is he _____?
5–6 Is your sister _____?
7–8 Is his hair _____?
9–10 Is their dog _____?
11–12 Is the train _____?

13–14 Is your friend _____?
15–16 Is the box _____?
17–18 Is the road _____?
19–20 Is her hair _____?
21–22 Is the tie _____?
23–24 Is the line _____?

25–26 Is the room _____?
27–28 Is the bridge _____?
29–30 Are the pants _____?
31–32 Are your neighbor's children _____?
33–34 Is the water _____?
35–36 Is your desk _____?

A. Tell me about your ....
B. He's/She's/It's/They're _____.

A. Do you have a/an _____ ....?
B. No. I have a/an _____ ....

Describe yourself.
Describe a person you know.
Describe some things in your home.
Describe some things in your community.

1–2	easy – difficult/hard		**19–20**	wet – dry
3–4	soft – hard		**21–22**	open – closed
5–6	clean – dirty		**23–24**	full – empty
7–8	smooth – rough		**25–26**	expensive – cheap/inexpensive
9–10	noisy/loud – quiet		**27–28**	fancy – plain
11–12	married – single		**29–30**	shiny – dull
13–14	rich/wealthy – poor		**31–32**	sharp – dull
15–16	pretty/beautiful – ugly		**33–34**	comfortable – uncomfortable
17–18	handsome – ugly		**35–36**	honest – dishonest

[1–2]
A. Is the homework **easy**?
B. No. It's **difficult**.

1–2 Is the homework _____?		**13–14** Is your uncle _____?		**25–26** Is that restaurant _____?
3–4 Is the mattress _____?		**15–16** Is the witch _____?		**27–28** Is the dress _____?
5–6 Are the windows _____?		**17–18** Is the pirate _____?		**29–30** Is your kitchen floor _____?
7–8 Is your skin _____?		**19–20** Are the clothes _____?		**31–32** Is the knife _____?
9–10 Is your neighbor _____?		**21–22** Is the door _____?		**33–34** Is the chair _____?
11–12 Is your sister _____?		**23–24** Is the pitcher _____?		**35–36** Is he _____?

A. Tell me about your ....
B. He's/She's/It's/They're _____.

A. Do you have a/an _____ ....?
B. No. I have a/an _____ ....

Describe yourself.
Describe a person you know.
Describe some things in your home.
Describe some things in your community.

1 tired
2 sleepy
3 exhausted
4 sick / ill

5 hot
6 cold
7 hungry
8 thirsty

9 full
10 happy
11 sad / unhappy
12 miserable

13 excited
14 disappointed
15 upset
16 annoyed

A. You look **tired**.
B. I am. I'm VERY **tired**.

What makes you happy?

What makes you sad?

When do you get annoyed?

1 angry/mad
2 furious
3 disgusted
4 frustrated

5 surprised
6 shocked
7 lonely
8 homesick

9 nervous
10 worried
11 scared/afraid
12 bored

13 proud
14 embarrassed
15 jealous
16 confused

A. Are you **angry**?
B. Yes. I'm VERY **angry**.

What makes you angry?

What makes you nervous?

Do you ever feel embarrassed? When?

1 apple
2 peach
3 pear
4 banana
5 plantain
6 plum

7 apricot
8 nectarine
9 kiwi
10 papaya
11 mango
12 fig
13 coconut

14 avocado
15 cantaloupe
16 honeydew (melon)
17 watermelon
18 pineapple
19 grapefruit

20 lemon
21 lime
22 orange
23 tangerine
24 grapes
25 cherries
26 prunes

27 dates
28 raisins
29 nuts
30 raspberries
31 blueberries
32 strawberries

[1–23]
A. This **apple** is delicious!
B. I'm glad you like it.

[24–32]
A. These **grapes** are delicious!
B. I'm glad you like them.

A. I'm hungry. Do we have any fruit?
B. Yes. We have _____s* and _____s.*

* With 15–19, use: We have _____ and _____.

A. Do we have any more _____s?†
B. No. I'll get some more when I go to the supermarket.

† With 15–19 use:
Do we have any more _____?

What are your favorite fruits?
Which fruits don't you like?

Which of these fruits grow where you live?

Name and describe other fruits you know.

VEGETABLES

1 celery
2 corn
3 broccoli
4 cauliflower
5 spinach
6 parsley
7 asparagus
8 eggplant
9 lettuce
10 cabbage

11 bok choy
12 zucchini
13 acorn squash
14 butternut squash
15 garlic
16 pea
17 string bean/
   green bean
18 lima bean
19 black bean
20 kidney bean

21 brussels sprout
22 cucumber
23 tomato
24 carrot
25 radish
26 mushroom
27 artichoke
28 potato
29 sweet potato
30 yam

31 green pepper/
   sweet pepper
32 red pepper
33 jalapeño (pepper)
34 chili pepper
35 beet
36 onion
37 scallion/green onion
38 turnip

A. What do we need from the supermarket?
B. We need **celery*** and **pea**s.†

* 1–15   † 16–38

A. How do you like the
   __[1–15]__ ?
B. It's delicious.

A. How do you like the
   __[16–38]__ s?
B. They're delicious.

Which vegetables do you like?
Which vegetables don't you like?

Which of these vegetables grow where you live?

Name and describe other vegetables you know.

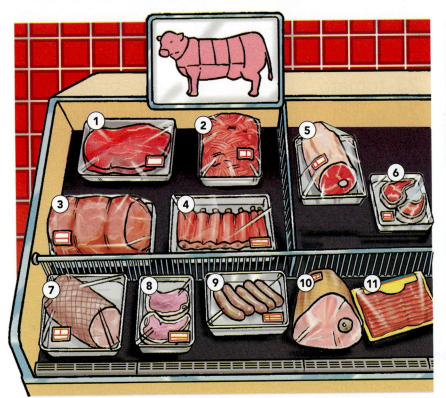

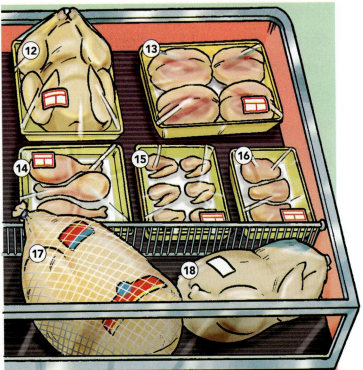

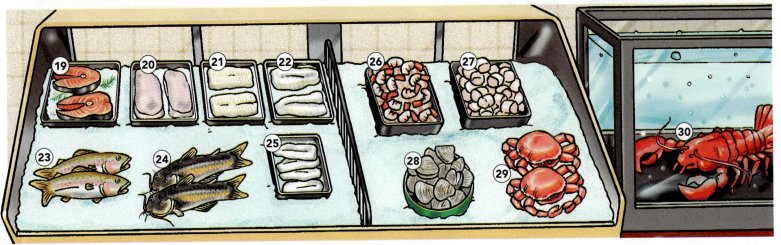

Meat

1 steak
2 ground beef
3 roast beef
4 ribs
5 leg of lamb
6 lamb chops
7 pork
8 pork chops
9 sausages
10 ham
11 bacon

Poultry

12 chicken
13 chicken breasts
14 chicken legs/ drumsticks
15 chicken wings
16 chicken thighs
17 turkey
18 duck

Seafood

FISH

19 salmon
20 halibut
21 haddock
22 flounder
23 trout
24 catfish
25 filet of sole

SHELLFISH

26 shrimp
27 scallops
28 clams
29 crabs
30 lobster

[1–11]

A. Excuse me. Where can I find **steak**?
B. Look in the Meat Section.
A. Thank you.

[12–18]

A. Excuse me. Where can I find **chicken**?
B. Look in the Poultry Section.
A. Thank you.

[19–30]

A. Excuse me. Where can I find **salmon**?
B. Look in the Seafood Section.
A. Thank you.

[1–3, 5, 7, 10–12, 17–25, 30]

A. This _____ looks very fresh!
B. Let's get some for dinner.

[4, 6, 8, 9, 13–16, 26–29]

A. These _____ look very fresh!
B. Let's get some for dinner.

Do you eat meat, poultry, or seafood? Which of these foods do you like?

Which of these foods are popular in your country?

Dairy Products

1 milk
2 low-fat milk
3 skim milk
4 chocolate milk
5 orange juice*
6 cheese
7 butter

8 margarine
9 sour cream
10 cream cheese
11 cottage cheese
12 yogurt
13 tofu*
14 eggs

* Orange juice and tofu are not dairy products, but they're usually found in this section.

Juices

15 apple juice
16 pineapple juice
17 grapefruit juice
18 tomato juice
19 grape juice
20 fruit punch

Beverages

21 soda
22 diet soda
23 bottled water

Coffee and Tea

24 coffee
25 decaffeinated coffee/decaf
26 instant coffee
27 tea
28 herbal tea
29 cocoa/ hot chocolate mix

A. I'm going to the supermarket to get some **milk**. Do we need anything else?
B. Yes. Please get some **apple juice**.

A. Excuse me. Where can I find _____ ?
B. Look in the _____ Section.
A. Thanks.

A. Look! _____ is on sale this week!
B. Let's get some!

* With 14, use: _____ are on sale this week.

Which of these foods do you like?

Which of these foods are good for you?

Which brands of these foods do you buy?

Deli

1 roast beef
2 bologna
3 salami
4 ham
5 turkey
6 corned beef

7 Swiss cheese
8 American cheese
9 mozzarella
10 cheddar cheese
11 potato salad
12 cole slaw

Frozen Foods

13 ice cream
14 frozen vegetables
15 frozen dinners
16 frozen lemonade
17 frozen orange juice

Snack Foods

18 potato chips
19 tortilla chips
20 pretzels
21 nuts
22 popcorn

A. Should we get some **roast beef**?
B. Good idea. And let's get some **potato salad**.

[1–12]
A. May I help you?
B. Yes, please. I'd like some _____.

[1–22]
A. Excuse me. Where is/are _____?
B. It's/They're in the _____ Section.

Which of these foods do you like?

Which brands of these foods do you buy?

Packaged Goods
1 cereal
2 cookies
3 crackers
4 macaroni
5 noodles
6 spaghetti
7 rice

Canned Goods
8 soup
9 tuna (fish)
10 (canned) vegetables
11 (canned) fruit

Jams and Jellies
12 jam
13 jelly
14 peanut butter

Condiments
15 ketchup
16 mustard
17 relish
18 pickles
19 olives
20 salt
21 pepper
22 spices
23 soy sauce
24 mayonnaise
25 (cooking) oil
26 olive oil
27 salsa
28 vinegar
29 salad dressing

Baked Goods
30 bread
31 rolls
32 English muffins
33 pita bread
34 cake

Baking Products
35 flour
36 sugar
37 cake mix

A. I got **cereal** and **soup**. What else is on the shopping list?
B. **Ketchup** and **bread**.

A. Excuse me. I'm looking for _____.
B. It's/They're next to the _____.

A. Pardon me. I'm looking for _____.
B. It's/They're between the _____ and the _____.

Which of these foods do you like?

Which brands of these foods do you buy?

Paper Products
1 napkins
2 paper cups
3 tissues
4 straws
5 paper plates
6 paper towels
7 toilet paper

Household Items
8 sandwich bags
9 trash bags
10 soap
11 liquid soap
12 aluminum foil
13 plastic wrap
14 waxed paper

Baby Products
15 baby cereal
16 baby food
17 formula
18 wipes
19 (disposable) diapers

Pet Food
20 cat food
21 dog food

A. Excuse me. Where can I find **napkins**?
B. **Napkins**? Look in Aisle 4.

[7, 10–17, 20, 21]
A. We forgot to get _____!
B. I'll get it. Where is it?
A. It's in Aisle _____.

[1–6, 8, 9, 18, 19]
A. We forgot to get _____!
B. I'll get them. Where are they?
A. They're in Aisle _____.

What do you need from the supermarket?
Make a complete shopping list!

1 aisle
2 shopper/customer
3 shopping basket
4 checkout line
5 checkout counter
6 cash register
7 shopping cart

8 coupons
9 cashier
10 paper bag
11 bagger/packer
12 express checkout (line)
13 scanner

14 plastic bag
15 manager
16 clerk
17 scale
18 can-return machine
19 bottle-return machine

A. This is a gigantic supermarket!
B. It is! Look at all the **aisle**s!

Where do you usually shop for food? Do you go to a supermarket, or do you go to a small grocery store? Describe the place where you shop.

Describe the differences between U.S. supermarkets and food stores in your country.

1 bag	**5** can	**9** head	**13** roll	**17** pint
2 bottle	**6** carton	**10** jar	**14** six-pack	**18** quart
3 box	**7** container	**11** loaf/loaves	**15** stick	**19** half-gallon
4 bunch	**8** dozen*	**12** package	**16** tube	**20** gallon
				21 liter
				22 pound

* "a dozen eggs," NOT "a dozen of eggs"

A. Please get a **bag** of *flour* when you go to the supermarket.
B. A **bag** of *flour*? Okay.

A. Please get two **bottles** of *ketchup* when you go to the supermarket.
B. Two **bottles** of *ketchup*? Okay.

[At home]
A. What did you get at the supermarket?
B. I got _____, _____, and _____.

[In a supermarket]
A. This is the express checkout line. Do you have more than eight items?
B. No. I only have _____, _____, and _____.

Open your kitchen cabinets and refrigerator. Make a list of all the things you find.

What do you do with empty bottles, jars, and cans? Do you recycle them, reuse them, or throw them away?

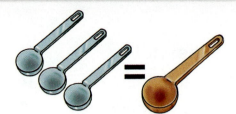

teaspoon
tsp.

tablespoon
Tbsp.

1 (fluid) ounce
1 fl. oz.

cup
c.
8 fl. ozs.

pint
pt.
16 fl. ozs.

quart
qt.
32 fl. ozs.

gallon
gal.
128 fl. ozs.

A. How much water should I put in?
B. The recipe says to add one _____ of water.

A. This fruit punch is delicious! What's in it?
B. Two _____s of apple juice, three _____s
of orange juice, and a _____ of grape juice.

an ounce

oz.

a quarter
of a pound
1/4 lb.
4 ozs.

half a pound

1/2 lb.
8 ozs.

three-quarters
of a pound
3/4 lb.
12 ozs.

a pound

lb.
16 ozs.

A. How much roast beef would you like?
B. I'd like _____, please.
A. Anything else?
B. Yes. Please give me _____ of Swiss cheese.

A. This chili tastes very good! What did you put in it?
B. _____ of ground beef, _____ of beans, _____ of tomatoes, and _____ of chili powder.

1 cut (up)
2 chop (up)
3 slice
4 grate
5 peel

6 break
7 beat
8 stir
9 pour
10 add

11 combine ___ and ___
12 mix ___ and ___
13 put ___ in ___
14 cook
15 bake

16 boil
17 broil
18 steam
19 fry
20 saute

21 simmer
22 roast
23 barbecue / grill
24 stir-fry
25 microwave

A. Can I help you?
B. Yes. Please **cut up** the vegetables.

[1–25]
A. What are you doing?
B. I'm _____ing the ....

[14–25]
A. How long should I _____ the ....?
B. _____ the .... for .... minutes / seconds.

What's your favorite recipe? Give instructions and use the units of measure on pages 114 and 115. For example:

Mix a cup of flour and two tablespoons of sugar.
Add half a pound of butter.
Bake at 350° (degrees) for twenty minutes.

1 hamburger
2 cheeseburger
3 hot dog
4 fish sandwich
5 chicken sandwich
6 fried chicken
7 french fries

8 nachos
9 taco
10 burrito
11 slice of pizza
12 bowl of chili
13 salad
14 ice cream

15 frozen yogurt
16 milkshake
17 soda
18 lids
19 paper cups
20 straws
21 napkins

22 plastic utensils
23 ketchup
24 mustard
25 mayonnaise
26 relish
27 salad dressing

A. May I help you?
B. Yes. I'd like a/an ___[1–5, 9–17]___ /
   an order of ___[6–8]___ .

A. Excuse me. We're almost out of ___[18–27]___ .
B. I'll get some more from the supply room.
   Thanks for telling me.

Do you go to fast-food restaurants? Which ones? How often? What do you order?

Are there fast-food restaurants in your country? Are they popular? What foods do they have?

1 donut
2 muffin
3 bagel
4 danish/pastry
5 biscuit
6 croissant

7 eggs
8 pancakes
9 waffles
10 toast
11 bacon
12 sausages

13 coffee
14 decaf coffee
15 tea
16 iced tea
17 lemonade
18 hot chocolate
19 milk

20 tuna fish sandwich
21 egg salad sandwich
22 chicken salad sandwich
23 ham and cheese sandwich
24 BLT/bacon, lettuce, and tomato sandwich

A. May I help you?
B. Yes. I'd like a ___[1–6]___/an order of ___[7–12]___, please.
A. Anything to drink?
B. Yes. I'll have a small/medium-size/large/extra-large ___[13–19]___.

A. I'd like a ___[20–24]___, please.
B. What do you want on it?
A. Lettuce/tomato/mayonnaise/mustard/. . .

Do you like these foods? Which ones? Where do you get them? How often do you have them?

A seat the customers
B pour the water
C take the order
D serve the meal

1 hostess
2 host
3 diner/customer
4 booth
5 table
6 high chair

7 booster seat
8 menu
9 bread basket
10 busperson
11 waitress/server
12 waiter/server

13 salad bar
14 dining room
15 kitchen
16 chef

[A–D]
A. Please **seat the customers**.
B. All right. I'll **seat the customers** right away.

[1, 2, 10–12, 16]
A. Do you have any job openings?
B. Yes. We're looking for a **hostess**.

[4–9]
A. Would you like a **booth**?
B. Yes, please.

[13–16]
A. This restaurant has a wonderful **salad bar**.
B. I agree.

Tell about a restaurant you know. Describe the place and the people. (Is the restaurant large or small? How many tables are there? How many people work there? Is there a salad bar? . . .)

A clear the table
B pay the check
C leave a tip
D set the table

1 dishroom
2 dishwasher
3 tray
4 dessert cart
5 check
6 tip

7 salad plate
8 bread-and-butter plate
9 dinner plate
10 soup bowl
11 water glass
12 wine glass
13 cup
14 saucer

15 napkin

silverware
16 salad fork
17 dinner fork
18 knife
19 teaspoon
20 soup spoon
21 butter knife

[A–D]
A. Please **clear the table**.
B. All right. I'll **clear the table** right away.

[7–21]
A. Excuse me. Where does the **salad fork** go?
B. It goes *to the left of* the **dinner fork**.

A. Excuse me. Where does the **bread-and-butter plate** go?
B. It goes *to the right of* the **salad plate**.

A. Excuse me. Where does the **cup** go?
B. It goes *on* the **saucer**.

A. Excuse me. Where does the **teaspoon** go?
B. It goes *between* the **knife** and the **soup spoon**.

Practice giving directions. Tell someone how to set a table. (Put the . . . . . .)

1. fruit cup
2. tomato juice
3. shrimp cocktail
4. chicken wings
5. nachos
6. potato skins

7. tossed salad
8. Greek salad
9. spinach salad
10. antipasto (plate)
11. Caesar salad

12. meatloaf
13. roast beef
14. baked chicken
15. broiled fish
16. spaghetti and meatballs
17. veal cutlet

18. a baked potato
19. mashed potatoes
20. french fries
21. rice
22. noodles
23. mixed vegetables

24. chocolate cake
25. apple pie
26. ice cream
27. jello
28. pudding
29. ice cream sundae

[Ordering dinner]

A. May I take your order?
B. Yes, please. For the appetizer, I'd like the ___[1–6]___ .
A. And what kind of salad would you like?
B. I'll have the ___[7–11]___ .
A. And for the main course?
B. I'd like the ___[12–17]___ , please.
A. What side dish would you like with that?
B. Hmm. I think I'll have ___[18–23]___ .

[Ordering dessert]

A. Would you like some dessert?
B. Yes. I'll have ___[24–28]___ /an ___[29]___ .

Tell about the food at a restaurant you know.
What's on the menu?

What are some typical foods on the menus of
restaurants in your country?

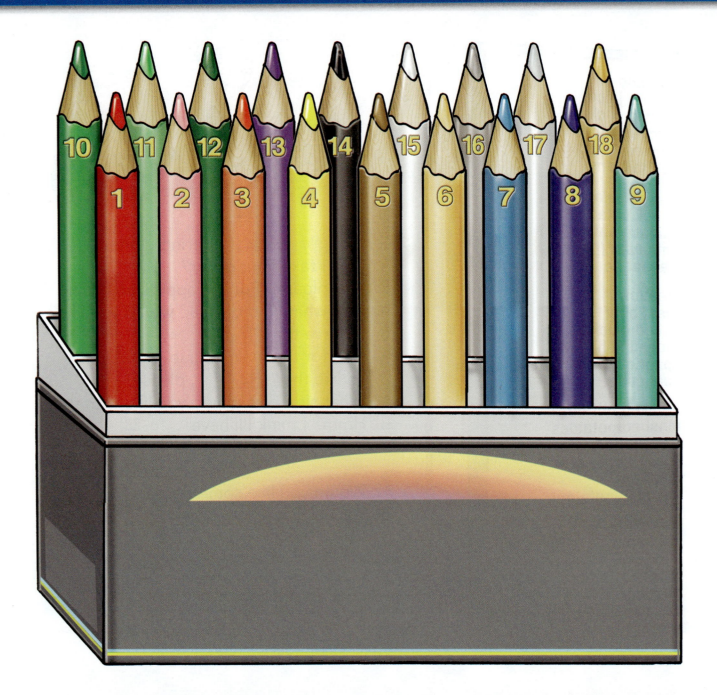

1 red
2 pink
3 orange
4 yellow
5 brown
6 beige
7 blue
8 navy blue
9 turquoise

10 green
11 light green
12 dark green
13 purple
14 black
15 white
16 gray
17 silver
18 gold

A. What's your favorite color?
B. **Red**.

A. I like your _____ shirt.
   You look very good in _____.
B. Thank you. _____ is my
   favorite color.

A. My TV is broken.
B. What's the matter with it?
A. People's faces are _____,
   the sky is _____, and the
   grass is _____!

Do you know the flags of different countries?
What are the colors of flags you know?

What color makes you happy? What color
makes you sad? Why?

1 blouse
2 skirt
3 shirt
4 pants/slacks
5 sport shirt
6 jeans
7 knit shirt/jersey
8 dress

9 sweater
10 jacket
11 sport coat/
   sport jacket
12 suit
13 three-piece
   suit
14 tie

15 uniform
16 T-shirt
17 shorts
18 maternity dress
19 jumpsuit
20 vest
21 jumper

22 tunic
23 leggings
24 overalls
25 turtleneck
26 tuxedo
27 bow tie
28 (evening) gown

A. I think I'll wear my new **blouse** today.
B. Good idea!

A. I really like your _____.
B. Thank you.
A. Where did you get it/them?
B. At ....

A. Oh, no! I just ripped
   my _____!
B. What a shame!

What clothing items in this lesson do you wear?

What color clothing do you like to wear?

What do you wear at work or at school? at parties? at weddings?

OUTERWEAR

1 coat
2 overcoat
3 hat
4 jacket
5 scarf
6 sweater jacket
7 tights

8 cap
9 leather jacket
10 baseball cap
11 windbreaker
12 raincoat
13 rain hat
14 trench coat

15 umbrella
16 poncho
17 rain jacket
18 rain boots
19 ski hat
20 ski jacket
21 gloves

22 ski mask
23 down jacket
24 mittens
25 parka
26 sunglasses
27 ear muffs
28 down vest

A. What's the weather like today?
B. It's cool/cold/raining/snowing.
A. I think I'll wear my _____.

[1–6, 8–17, 19, 20, 22, 23, 25, 28]
A. May I help you?
B. Yes, please. I'm looking for a/an _____.

[7, 18, 21, 24, 26, 27]
A. May I help you?
B. Yes, please. I'm looking for _____.

What do you wear outside when the weather is cool?/when it's raining?/when it's very cold?

1 pajamas
2 nightgown
3 nightshirt
4 bathrobe
5 slippers
6 blanket sleeper

7 undershirt
8 underpants
9 boxer shorts
10 athletic supporter/jockstrap
11 long underwear
12 socks

13 panties
14 briefs/
   underpants
15 bra
16 camisole
17 slip

18 stockings
19 pantyhose
20 tights
21 knee socks

A. I can't find my new _____.
B. Did you look in the bureau/dresser/closet?
A. Yes, I did.
B. Then it's/they're probably in the wash.

What sleepwear items do you wear? What sleepwear items do people in your family wear?

1 tank top
2 running shorts
3 sweatband
4 jogging suit
5 T-shirt
6 lycra shorts/bike shorts
7 sweatshirt
8 sweatpants
9 cover-up
10 swimsuit/bathing suit
11 swimming trunks/swimsuit/bathing suit
12 leotard

13 shoes
14 (high) heels
15 sneakers
16 tennis shoes
17 running shoes
18 high-tops/high-top sneakers
19 sandals
20 thongs/flip-flops
21 boots
22 work boots

[1–12]
A. Excuse me. I found this/these _____ in the dryer. Is it/Are they yours?
B. Yes. It's/They're mine. Thank you.

[13–22]
A. Are those new _____?
B. Yes, they are.
A. They're very nice.
B. Thanks.

Do you exercise? What do you do? What kind of clothing do you wear when you exercise?

What kind of shoes do you wear when you go to work or to school? when you exercise?
when you relax at home? when you go out with friends or family members?

1 ring
2 engagement ring
3 wedding ring / wedding band
4 earrings
5 necklace
6 pearl necklace / pearls
7 chain
8 beads
9 pin
10 locket
11 bracelet
12 barrette
13 cuff links

14 suspenders
15 watch
16 handkerchief
17 key ring
18 change purse
19 wallet
20 belt
21 purse / handbag / pocketbook
22 shoulder bag
23 book bag
24 backpack
25 makeup bag
26 briefcase

A. Oh, no! I think I lost my **ring**!
B. I'll help you look for it.

A. Oh, no! I think I lost my **earrings**!
B. I'll help you look for them.

[In a store]
A. Excuse me. Is this / Are these _____ on sale this week?
B. Yes. It's / They're half price.

[On the street]
A. Help! Police! Stop that man / woman!
B. What happened?!
A. He / She just stole my _____ and my _____!

Do you like to wear jewelry? What jewelry do you have?

In your country, what do men, women, and children use to carry their things?

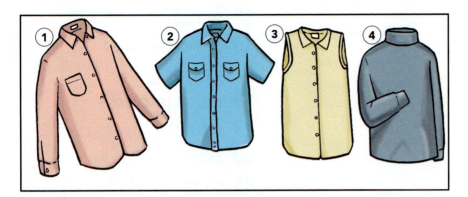

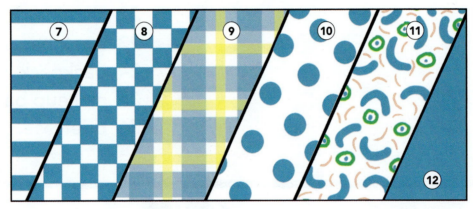

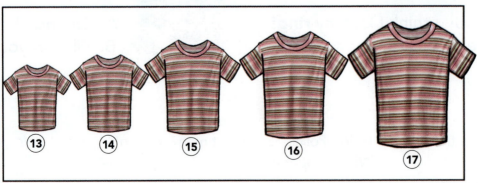

Types of Clothing
1 long-sleeved shirt
2 short-sleeved shirt
3 sleeveless shirt
4 turtleneck (shirt)

5 pierced earrings
6 clip-on earrings

Patterns
7 striped
8 checked
9 plaid
10 polka-dotted
11 print
12 solid *blue*

Sizes
13 extra-small
14 small
15 medium
16 large
17 extra-large

[1–4]
A. May I help you?
B. Yes, please. I'm looking for a *shirt.*
A. What kind?
B. I'm looking for a *long-sleeved shirt.*

[7–12]
A. How do you like this _____ tie/shirt/skirt?
B. Actually, I prefer that _____ one.

[13–17]
A. What size are you looking for?
B. _____.

Describe your favorite clothing items. For each item, tell about the color, the size, and the pattern.

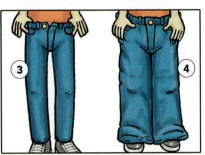

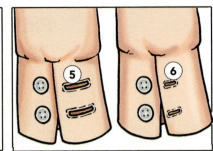

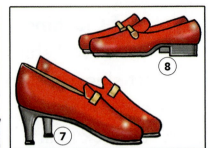

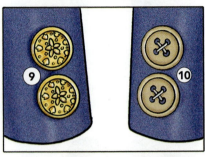

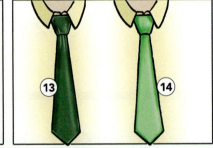

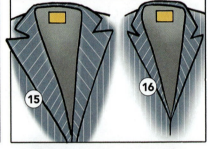

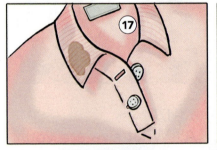

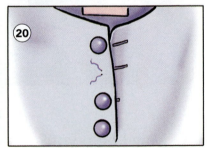

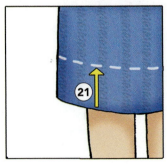

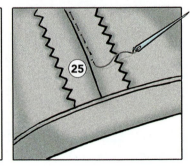

1–2 long – short
3–4 tight – loose/baggy
5–6 large/big – small
7–8 high – low
9–10 fancy – plain
11–12 heavy – light
13–14 dark – light
15–16 wide – narrow

17 stained *collar*
18 ripped/torn *pocket*
19 broken *zipper*
20 missing *button*
21 shorten the *skirt*
22 lengthen the *sleeves*
23 take in the *jacket*
24 let out the *pants*
25 fix/repair the *seam*

[1–2]
A. Are the sleeves too **long**?
B. No. They're too **short**.

1–2 Are the sleeves too _____?
3–4 Are the pants too _____?
5–6 Are the buttonholes too _____?
7–8 Are the heels too _____?

9–10 Are the buttons too _____?
11–12 Is the coat too _____?
13–14 Is the color too _____?
15–16 Are the lapels too _____?

[17–20]
A. What's the matter with it?
B. It has a **stained** *collar*.

[21–25]
A. Please **shorten** the *skirt*.
B. **Shorten** the *skirt*? Okay.

Tell about the differences between clothing people wear now and clothing people wore a long time ago.

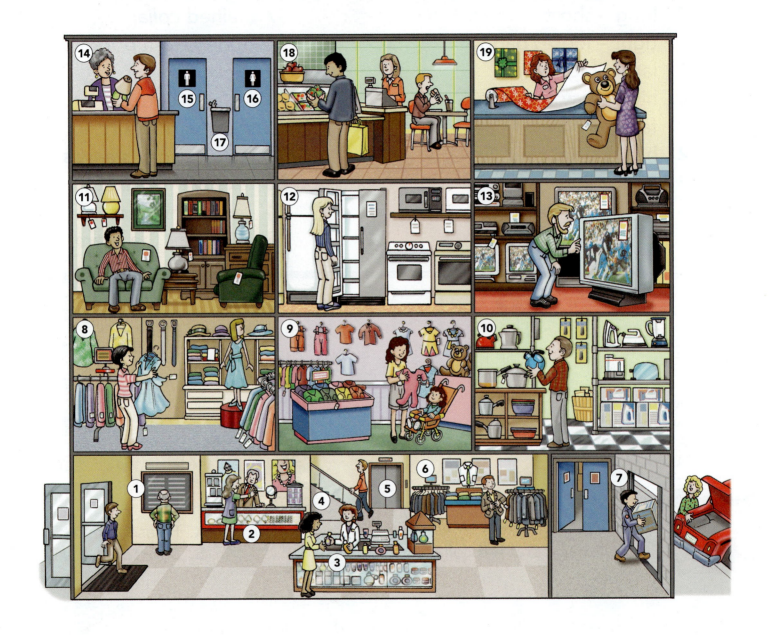

1 (store) directory
2 Jewelry Counter
3 Perfume Counter
4 escalator
5 elevator
6 Men's Clothing Department
7 customer pickup area
8 Women's Clothing Department
9 Children's Clothing Department
10 Housewares Department

11 Furniture Department
12 Household Appliances Department
13 Electronics Department
14 Customer Service Counter
15 men's room
16 ladies' room
17 water fountain
18 snack bar
19 Gift Wrap Counter

A. Excuse me. Where's the **store directory**?
B. It's over there, next to the **Jewelry Counter**.
A. Thanks.
B. You're welcome.

A. Excuse me. Do you sell *ties**?
B. Yes. You can find *ties** in the ___[6, 8–13]___ /at the ___[2, 3]___.
A. Thank you.

**ties/bracelets/dresses/toasters/. . .*

Describe a department store you know. Tell what is on each floor.

A buy
B return
C exchange
D try on
E pay for
F get some information about

1 sale sign
2 label
3 price tag
4 receipt

5 discount
6 size
7 material
8 care instructions

9 regular price
10 sale price
11 price
12 sales tax
13 total price

A. May I help you?
B. Yes, please. I want to ___[A–F]___ this item.
A. Certainly. I'll be glad to help you.

A. {What's the ___[5–7, 9–13]___ ?
{What are the ___[8]___ ?
B. _____.
A. Are you sure?
B. Yes. Look at the ___[1–4]___ !

Which stores in your area have sales? How often?

Tell about something you bought on sale.

1 TV/television
2 DVD
3 DVD player
4 video/videotape
5 VCR
6 camcorder/video camera
7 radio
8 clock radio
9 tape recorder
10 microphone

11 stereo system/ sound system
12 CD
13 CD player
14 audiotape
15 tape deck
16 speakers
17 portable stereo system/ boombox
18 personal CD player

19 personal cassette player
20 headphones
21 personal digital audio player
22 video game system
23 video game
24 telephone/phone
25 cell phone
26 answering machine

27 calculator
28 (35 millimeter) camera
29 lens
30 film
31 digital camera
32 memory disk
33 flash (attachment)

A. May I help you?
B. Yes, please. I'm looking for a **TV**.

* With 16, 20, 30, use: I'm looking for _____.

A. Excuse me. Do you sell _____(s)?*
B. Yes. We have a large selection of _____s.

* With 30, use: Do you sell _____?

A. I like your new _____.
   Where did you get it/them?
B. At ......(name of store)........

What equipment in this lesson do you have or want?

In your opinion, which brands of equipment are the best?

Computer Hardware

1 (desktop) computer
2 CPU/central processing unit
3 monitor/screen
4 CD-ROM drive
5 CD-ROM
6 disk drive
7 (floppy) disk
8 keyboard
9 mouse

10 flat panel screen/ LCD screen
11 notebook computer
12 joystick
13 track ball
14 modem
15 surge protector
16 printer
17 scanner
18 cable

Computer Software

19 word-processing program
20 spreadsheet program
21 educational software program
22 computer game

A. Can you recommend a good **computer**?
B. Yes. This **computer** here is excellent.

A. Is that a new _____?
B. Yes.
A. Where did you get it?
B. At ......_(name of store)_...... .

A. May I help you?
B. Yes, please. Do you sell _____s?
A. Yes. We carry a complete line of _____s.

Do you use a computer? When?

In your opinion, why are computers important?

A make a deposit
B make a withdrawal
C cash a check
D get traveler's checks
E open an account
F apply for a loan
G exchange currency

1 deposit slip
2 withdrawal slip
3 check
4 traveler's check
5 bankbook
6 ATM card
7 credit card

8 (bank) vault
9 safe deposit box
10 teller
11 security guard
12 ATM (machine)/ cash machine
13 bank officer

[A–G]
A. Where are you going?
B. I'm going to the bank. I have to _____.

[5–7]
A. What are you looking for?
B. My _____. I can't find it anywhere!

[8–13]
A. How many _____s does the State Street Bank have?
B. ....

Do you have a bank account? What kind? Where? What do you do at the bank?

Do you ever use traveler's checks? When?

Do you have a credit card? What kind? When do you use it?

FINANCES

Forms of Payment

1 cash
2 check
3 credit card
4 money order
5 traveler's check

Household Bills

6 rent
7 mortgage payment
8 electric bill
9 telephone bill
10 gas bill
11 oil bill/heating bill
12 water bill
13 cable TV bill
14 car payment
15 credit card bill

Family Finances

16 balance the checkbook
17 write a check
18 bank online
19 checkbook
20 check register
21 monthly statement

Using an ATM Machine

22 insert the ATM card
23 enter your PIN* number
24 select a transaction
25 make a deposit
26 withdraw/get cash
27 transfer funds
28 remove your card
29 take your receipt

* personal identification number

A. Can I pay by __[1, 2]__ / with a __[3–5]__ ?
B. Yes, you can.

A. What are you doing?
B. { I'm paying the __[6–15]__ .
{ I'm __[16–18]__ ing.

A. What are you doing?
B. I'm looking for the __[19–21]__ .

A. What should I do?
B. __[22–29]__ .

What household bills do you receive? How much do you pay for the different bills?

Who takes care of the finances in your household? What does that person do?

Do you use ATM machines? If you do, how do you use them?

1 letter
2 postcard
3 air letter
4 package
5 first class
6 priority mail
7 express mail
8 parcel post
9 certified mail

10 stamp
11 sheet of stamps
12 roll of stamps
13 book of stamps
14 money order
15 change-of-address form
16 selective service registration form

17 passport application form
18 envelope
19 return address
20 mailing address
21 zip code
22 stamp
23 mail slot

24 postal worker/ postal clerk
25 scale
26 stamp machine
27 letter carrier/ mail carrier
28 mail truck
29 mailbox

[1–4]
A. Where are you going?
B. To the post office. I have to mail a/an _____.

[5–9]
A. How do you want to send it?
B. _____, please.

[10–17]
A. Next!
B. I'd like a _____, please.
A. Here you are.

[19–22]
A. Do you want me to mail this letter?
B. Yes, thanks.
A. Oops! You forgot the _____!

How often do you go to the post office? What do you do there?

Tell about the postal system in your country.

THE LIBRARY

1 online catalog
2 card catalog
3 library card
4 copier
5 shelves
6 children's section
7 children's books
8 periodical section
9 magazines
10 newspapers

11 media section
12 books on tape
13 audiotapes
14 CDs
15 videotapes
16 (computer) software
17 DVDs
18 foreign language section
19 foreign language books
20 reference section

21 microfilm reader
22 dictionary
23 encyclopedia
24 atlas
25 reference desk
26 (reference) librarian
27 checkout desk
28 library clerk

[1, 2, 4–28]
A. Excuse me. Where's/Where are the _____?
B. Over there.

[22–24]
A. Excuse me. Where can I find a/an _____?
B. Look in the reference section.
A. Thank you.

[6–12, 17–20]
A. Can you help me? I'm looking for [7, 9, 10, 12, 17, 19] .
B. Look in the [6, 8, 11, 18, 20] over there.
A. Thanks.

Do you go to a library? Where? What does this library have?

Tell about how you use the library.

A
1
2
3
B
4
5
C
6
7
8
D
Martin Jones
9
10
E
11
12
13
14
F
15
16
G
17
18
19
H
20
I
J
K
L

A police station
B fire station
C hospital
D town hall/city hall
E recreation center
F dump
G child-care center
H senior center
I church
J synagogue
K mosque
L temple

1 emergency operator
2 police officer
3 police car
4 fire engine
5 firefighter
6 emergency room
7 EMT/paramedic
8 ambulance
9 mayor/city manager
10 meeting room

11 gym
12 activities director
13 game room
14 swimming pool
15 sanitation worker
16 recycling center
17 child-care worker
18 nursery
19 playroom
20 eldercare worker/
      senior care worker

[A–L]
A. Where are you going?
B. I'm going to the _____.

[1, 2, 5, 7, 12, 15, 17, 20]
A. What do you do?
B. I'm a/an _____.

[3, 4, 8]
A. Do you hear a siren?
B. Yes. There's a/an _____
   coming up behind us.

What community institutions are in your city or town? Where are they located?

Which community institutions do you use? When?

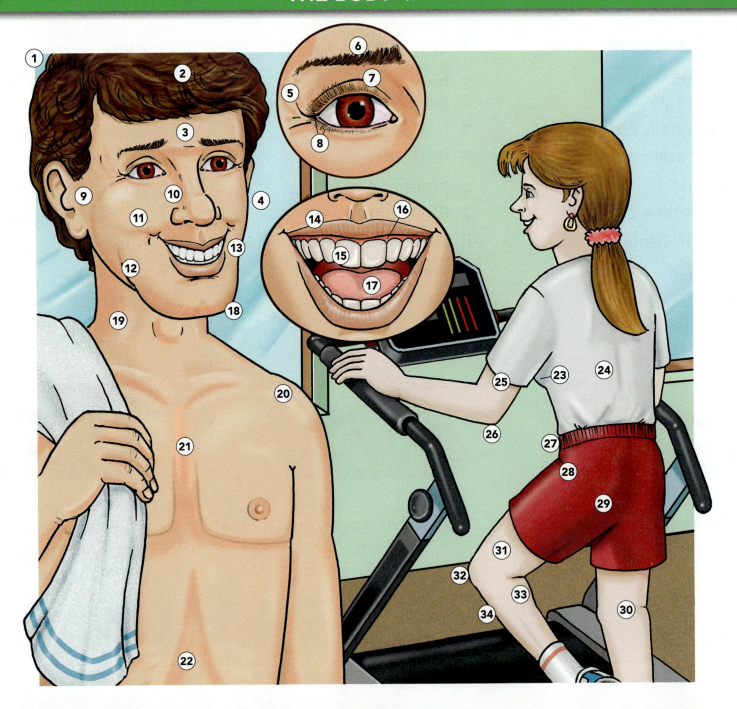

1 head	8 eyelashes	15 tooth–teeth	22 abdomen	29 buttocks
2 hair	9 ear	16 gums	23 breast	30 leg
3 forehead	10 nose	17 tongue	24 back	31 thigh
4 face	11 cheek	18 chin	25 arm	32 knee
5 eye	12 jaw	19 neck	26 elbow	33 calf
6 eyebrow	13 mouth	20 shoulder	27 waist	34 shin
7 eyelid	14 lip	21 chest	28 hip	

A. My doctor checked my **head** and said everything is okay.
B. I'm glad to hear that.

[1, 3–7, 9–26, 28–34]
A. Ooh!
B. What's the matter?
{ My _____ hurts!
{ My _____s hurt!

A. Doctor's Office.
B. Hello. This is ....(name)..... .
I'm concerned about my _____.
A. Do you want to make an appointment?
B. Yes, please.

Describe yourself as completely as you can.

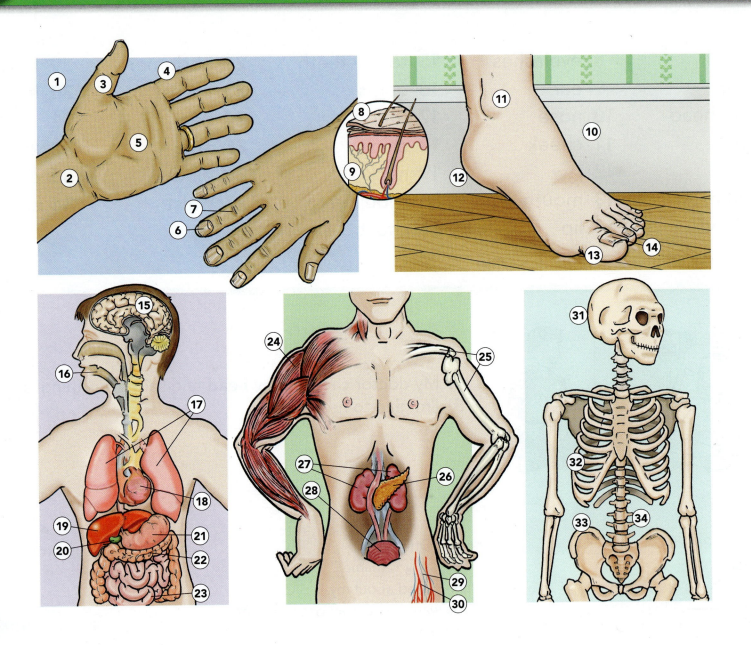

1 hand
2 wrist
3 thumb
4 finger
5 palm
6 fingernail
7 knuckle
8 skin

9 nerve
10 foot
11 ankle
12 heel
13 toe
14 toenail
15 brain
16 throat

17 lungs
18 heart
19 liver
20 gallbladder
21 stomach
22 large intestine
23 small intestine

24 muscles
25 bones
26 pancreas
27 kidneys
28 bladder
29 veins
30 arteries

31 skull
32 ribcage
33 pelvis
34 spinal column/
    spinal cord

[1–7, 10–14]
A. What's the matter?
B. I hurt my **hand**.

[1–14]
A. Does your **wrist** hurt
    when I do THIS?
B. Yes, it does.

[8, 15–34]
A. How am I, Doctor?
B. Well, I'm a little concerned
    about your **skin**.

Which parts of the body on pages 162–165 are most important at school? at work?
when you play your favorite sport?

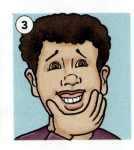

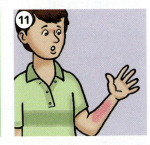

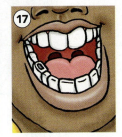

1 headache
2 earache
3 toothache
4 stomachache
5 backache
6 sore throat

7 fever/temperature
8 cold
9 cough
10 infection
11 rash
12 insect bite

13 sunburn
14 stiff neck
15 runny nose
16 bloody nose
17 cavity
18 blister
19 wart

20 (the) hiccups
21 (the) chills
22 cramps
23 diarrhea
24 chest pain
25 shortness of breath
26 laryngitis

A. What's the matter?
B. I have a/an ___[1–19]___ .

A. What's the matter?
B. I have ___[20–26]___ .

A. How do you feel?
B. Not so good.
A. What's the matter?
B. ....
A. I'm sorry to hear that.

A. Are you okay?
B. Not really. I don't feel very well.
A. What's wrong?
B. ....
A. I'm sorry to hear that.

Tell about a time you had one of these problems.

What do you do when you have a cold? a stomachache? an insect bite? the hiccups?

1 faint	**6** exhausted	**11** vomit / throw up	**16** bruise	**20** sprain
2 dizzy	**7** cough	**12** bleed	**17** burn	**21** dislocate
3 nauseous	**8** sneeze	**13** twist	**18** hurt–hurt	**22** break–broke
4 bloated	**9** wheeze	**14** scratch	**19** cut–cut	**23** swollen
5 congested	**10** burp	**15** scrape		**24** itchy

A. What's the problem?

B. { I feel ___[1–4]___.
    I'm ___[5, 6]___.

A. Can you describe your symptoms?

B. I'm ___[7–12]___ing a lot.

A. What happened?

B. { I ___[13–19]___ my ....
    I think I ___[20–22]___ed my ....
    My .... is/are ___[23, 24]___.

Tell about the last time you didn't feel well. What was the matter?

Tell about a time you hurt yourself. What happened? How? What did you do about it?

FIRST AID

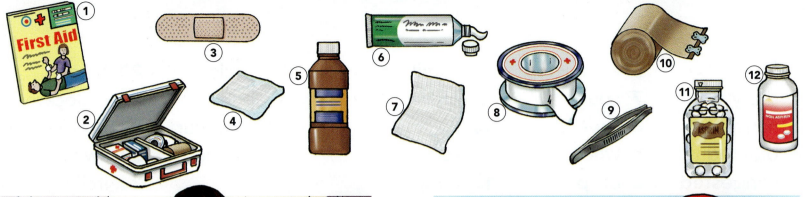

1 First Aid
2
3
4
5
6
7
8
9
10
11
12

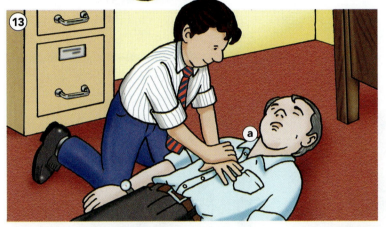

13 a

14 b

15 c

16 d

17 e

1 first-aid manual
2 first-aid kit
3 bandage/Band-Aid™
4 sterile (dressing) pad
5 hydrogen peroxide
6 antibiotic ointment
7 gauze
8 adhesive tape
9 tweezers
10 elastic bandage/Ace™ bandage
11 aspirin
12 non-aspirin pain reliever

13 CPR*
  a has no pulse
14 rescue breathing
  b isn't breathing
15 the Heimlich maneuver
  c is choking
16 splint
  d broke a finger
17 tourniquet
  e is bleeding

* cardiopulmonary resuscitation

A. Do we have any ___[3, 4, 10]___ s/
   ___[5–9, 11, 12]___ ?
B. Yes. Look in the first-aid kit.

A. Help! My friend ___[a-e]___ !
B. I can help!
  { I know how to do ___[13-15]___ .
  { I can make a ___[16, 17]___ .

Do you have a first-aid kit? If you do, what's in it? If you don't, where can you buy one?

Tell about a time when you gave or received first aid.

Where can a person learn first aid in your community?

1 hurt/injured
2 in shock
3 unconscious
4 heatstroke
5 frostbite
6 heart attack
7 allergic reaction
8 swallow poison
9 overdose on drugs

10 fall–fell
11 get–got an electric shock
12 the flu/influenza
13 an ear infection
14 strep throat
15 measles
16 mumps
17 chicken pox
18 asthma

19 cancer
20 depression
21 diabetes
22 heart disease
23 high blood pressure/
   hypertension
24 TB/tuberculosis
25 AIDS*

* Acquired Immune Deficiency
  Syndrome

A. What's the matter?
B. My .... { is ___[1–3]___ .
                   { has ___[4, 5]___ .
                   { is having a/an ___[6, 7]___ .
A. What's your address?
B. ___(address)___ .

A. What happened?
B. My .... ___[8–11]___ ed.
A. What's your location?
B. ___(address)___ in ___(city/town)___ .

A. My .... is sick.
B. What's the matter?
A. He/She has ___[12–25]___ .
B. I'm sorry to hear that.

Tell about a medical emergency that happened to you or someone you know.

Which illnesses in this lesson are you familiar with?

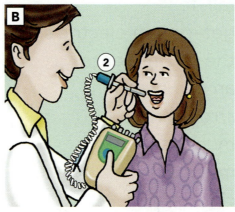

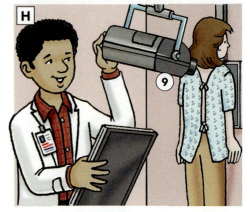

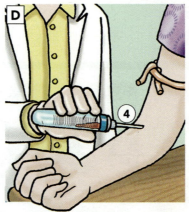

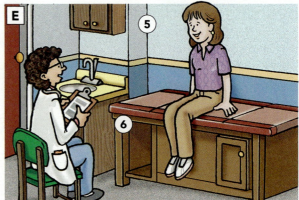

A measure *your* height and weight
B take *your* temperature
C check *your* blood pressure
D draw some blood
E ask *you* some questions about *your* health
F examine *your* eyes, ears, nose, and throat
G listen to *your* heart
H take a chest X-ray

1 scale
2 thermometer
3 blood pressure gauge
4 needle
5 examination room
6 examination table
7 eye chart
8 stethoscope
9 X-ray machine

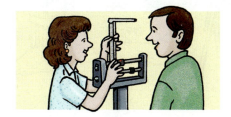

[A–H]
A. Now I'm going to **measure your height and weight**.
B. All right.

[A–H]
A. What did the doctor/nurse do during the examination?
B. She/He **measured my height and weight**.

[1–3, 5–9]
A. So, how do you like our new **scale?**
B. It's very nice, doctor.

How often do you have a medical exam?

What does the doctor/nurse do?

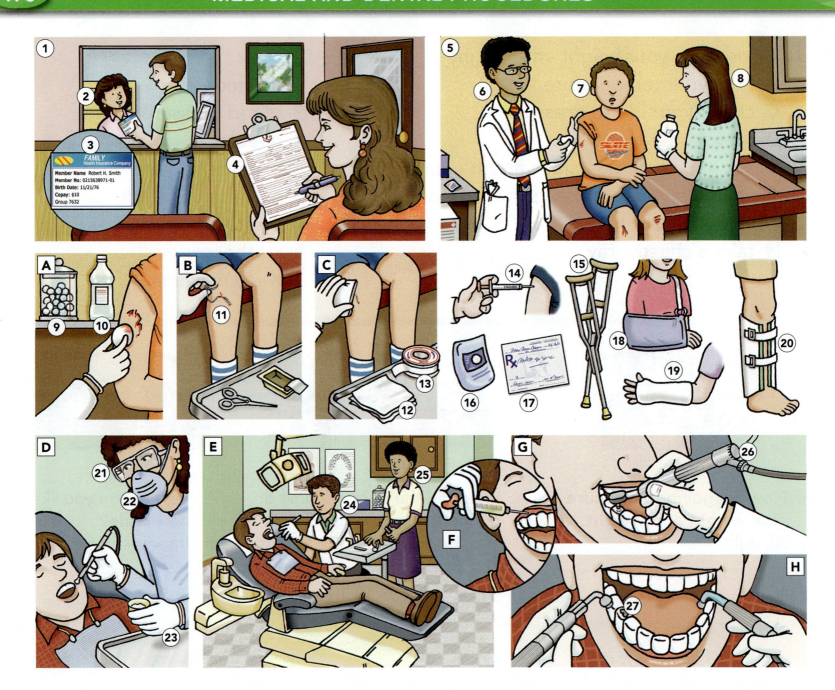

FAMILY
Health Insurance Company
Member Name   Robert H. Smith
Member No: 0215638971-01
Birth Date: 11/21/76
Copay: $10
Group 7632

A clean the wound
B close the wound
C dress the wound
D clean *your* teeth
E examine *your* teeth
F give *you* a shot of anesthetic/Novocaine™
G drill the cavity
H fill the tooth

1 waiting room
2 receptionist
3 insurance card
4 medical history form
5 examination room
6 doctor/physician
7 patient
8 nurse
9 cotton balls

10 alcohol
11 stitches
12 gauze
13 tape
14 injection/ shot
15 crutches
16 ice pack
17 prescription
18 sling

19 cast
20 brace
21 hygienist
22 mask
23 gloves
24 dentist
25 dental assistant
26 drill
27 filling

A. Now I'm going to ___[A–H]___.
B. Will it hurt?
A. Just a little.

A. I'm going to { give you (a/an) ___[14–17]___.
              { put your ....in ___[18–20]___.
B. Okay.

A. I need { ___[9, 10, 12, 13, 23]___.
          { a ___[22, 26]___.
B. Here you are.

Tell about a personal experience you had with a medical or dental procedure.

ANNA LOPEZ

EAR NOSE
& THROAT

NORTH
BEACH
DIET

1 rest in bed
2 drink fluids
3 gargle
4 go on a diet

5 exercise
6 take vitamins
7 see a specialist
8 get acupuncture

9 heating pad
10 humidifier
11 air purifier
12 cane
13 walker
14 wheelchair

15 blood work / blood tests
16 tests
17 physical therapy
18 surgery
19 counseling
20 braces

A. I think you should ___[1–8]___ .
B. I understand.

A. I think { you should use a/an ___[9–14]___ .
            { you need ___[15–20]___ .
B. I see.

A. What did the doctor say?

B. The doctor thinks { I should ___[1–8]___ .
                      { I should use a/an ___[9–14]___ .
                      { I need ___[15–20]___ .

Tell about medical advice a doctor gave you. What did the doctor say? Did you follow the advice?

1 aspirin
2 cold tablets
3 vitamins
4 cough syrup
5 non-aspirin pain reliever

6 cough drops
7 throat lozenges
8 antacid tablets
9 decongestant spray/ nasal spray

10 eye drops
11 ointment
12 cream/creme
13 lotion

14 pill
15 tablet
16 capsule
17 caplet
18 teaspoon
19 tablespoon

A. What did the doctor say?
B. She told me to take ___[1–4]___ /a ___[5]___ .

A. What did the doctor recommend?
B. He told me to use ___[6–13]___ .

[14–19]
A. What's the dosage?
B. One _____ every four hours.

What medicines in this lesson do you have at home? What other medicines do you have?

What do you take or use for a fever? a headache? a stomachache? a sore throat? a cold? a cough?

Tell about any medicines in your country that are different from the ones in this lesson.

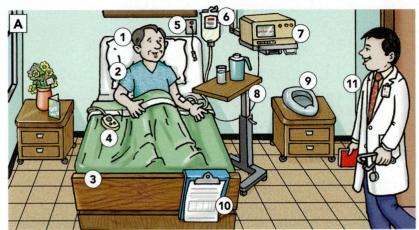

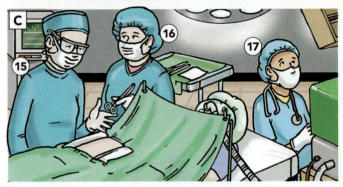

A patient's room
1 patient
2 hospital gown
3 hospital bed
4 bed control
5 call button
6 I.V.
7 vital signs monitor
8 bed table
9 bed pan
10 medical chart
11 doctor/physician

B nurse's station
12 nurse
13 dietitian
14 orderly

C operating room
15 surgeon
16 surgical nurse
17 anesthesiologist

D waiting room
18 volunteer

E birthing room/delivery room
19 obstetrician
20 midwife/nurse-midwife

F emergency room/ER
21 emergency medical technician/EMT
22 gurney

G radiology department
23 X-ray technician
24 radiologist

H laboratory/lab
25 lab technician

A. This is your ___[2–10]___.
B. I see.

A. Do you work here?
B. Yes. I'm a/an ___[11–21, 23–25]___.

A. Where's the ___[11–21, 23–25]___?
B. She's/He's { in the ___[A, C–H]___.
              at the ___[B]___.

Tell about an experience you or a family member had in the hospital.

A   1   2

B   3

C   4

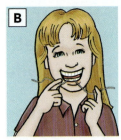

D   5   6

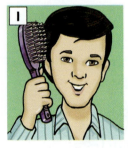

E   7

F   8   9

G   10

H   11

I   12

J   13   14   15

K   16   17   18   19

L   20   21   22   23

M   24   25   26   27   28

N   29   30

A brush *my* teeth
1 toothbrush
2 toothpaste

B floss *my* teeth
3 dental floss

C gargle
4 mouthwash

D bathe/take a bath
5 soap
6 bubble bath

E take a shower
7 shower cap

F wash *my* hair
8 shampoo
9 conditioner

G dry *my* hair
10 hair dryer/
     blow dryer

H comb *my* hair
11 comb

I brush *my* hair
12 brush

J shave
13 shaving cream
14 razor
15 electric shaver

K do *my* nails
16 nail file
17 nail clipper
18 scissors
19 nail polish

L put on . . .
20 deodorant
21 cologne/perfume

22 powder
23 sunscreen

M put on makeup
24 blush/rouge
25 eyeliner
26 eye shadow
27 mascara
28 lipstick

N polish *my* shoes
29 shoe polish
30 shoelaces

[A–K, L (20–23), M, N]
A. What are you doing?
B. I'm _____ing.

[1, 7, 10–12, 14–18, 30]
A. Excuse me. Where can I find _____(s)?
B. They're in the next aisle.

[2–6, 8, 9, 13, 19–29]
A. Excuse me. Where can I find _____?
B. It's in the next aisle.

Which of these personal care products do you use?

You're going on a trip. Make a list of the personal care products you need to take with you.

A feed
1 baby food
2 bib
3 bottle
4 nipple
5 formula
6 (liquid) vitamins

B change the baby's diaper
7 disposable diaper
8 cloth diaper
9 diaper pin
10 (baby) wipes

11 baby powder
12 training pants
13 ointment

C bathe
14 baby shampoo
15 cotton swab
16 baby lotion

D hold
17 pacifier
18 teething ring

E nurse

F dress

G rock
19 child-care center
20 child-care worker
21 rocking chair

H read to
22 cubby

I play with
23 toys

A. What are you doing?
B. { I'm _____[A, C–I]_____ing the baby.
     I'm ___[B]___ing.

A. Do we need anything from the store?
B. Yes. We need some more { _____[2–4, 7–9, 15, 17, 18]_____s.
                              _____[1, 5, 6, 10–14, 16]_____.

In your opinion, which are better: cloth diapers or disposable diapers? Why?

Tell about baby products in your country.

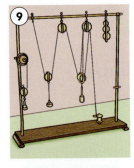

1 math / mathematics
2 English
3 history
4 geography
5 government
6 science
7 biology
8 chemistry
9 physics
10 health

11 computer science
12 Spanish
13 French
14 home economics
15 industrial arts / shop
16 business education
17 physical education / P.E.
18 driver's education / driver's ed
19 art
20 music

A. What do you have next period?
B. **Math**. How about you?
A. **English**.
B. There's the bell. I've got to go.

What is/was your favorite subject? Why?

In your opinion, what's the most interesting subject? the most difficult subject? Why do you think so?

1 band
2 orchestra
3 choir / chorus
4 drama
5 football
6 cheerleading / pep squad
7 student government
8 community service

9 school newspaper
10 yearbook
11 literary magazine
12 A.V. crew
13 debate club
14 computer club
15 international club
16 chess club

[1–6]
A. Are you going home right after school?
B. No. I have **band** practice.

[7–16]
A. What are you going to do after school today?
B. I have a **student government** meeting.

What extracurricular activities do / did you participate in?

Which extracurricular activities in this lesson are there in schools in your country? What other activities are there?

Arithmetic

$$2+1=3 \qquad 8-3=5 \qquad 4\times2=8 \qquad 10\div2=5$$

addition	subtraction	multiplication	division
2 **plus** 1 **equals*** 3.	8 **minus** 3 **equals*** 5.	4 **times** 2 **equals*** 8.	10 **divided by** 2 **equals*** 5.

* You can also say: **is**

A. How much is *two plus one?*
B. *Two plus one* equals / is *three.*

Make conversations for the arithmetic problems above and others.

Fractions

1/4	1/3	1/2	2/3	3/4
one quarter / one fourth	one third	one half / half	two thirds	three quarters / three fourths

A. Is this on sale?
B. Yes. It's _____ off the regular price.

A. Is the gas tank almost empty?
B. It's about _____ full.

Percents

10%
ten
percent

50%
fifty
percent

75%
seventy-five
percent

100%
one-hundred
percent

A. How did you do on the test?
B. I got _____ percent of the answers right.

A. What's the weather forecast?
B. There's a _____ percent chance of rain.

Types of Math

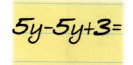
$5y-5y+3=$

algebra

geometry

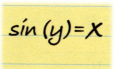
$\sin(y)=x$

trigonometry

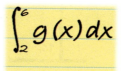
$\int_{2}^{6} g(x)\,dx$

calculus

statistics

A. What math course are you taking this year?
B. I'm taking _____.

Are you good at math?

What math courses do/did you take in school?

Tell about something you bought on sale. How much off the regular price was it?

Research and discuss: What percentage of people in your country live in cities? live on farms? work in factories?

MEASUREMENTS AND GEOMETRIC SHAPES

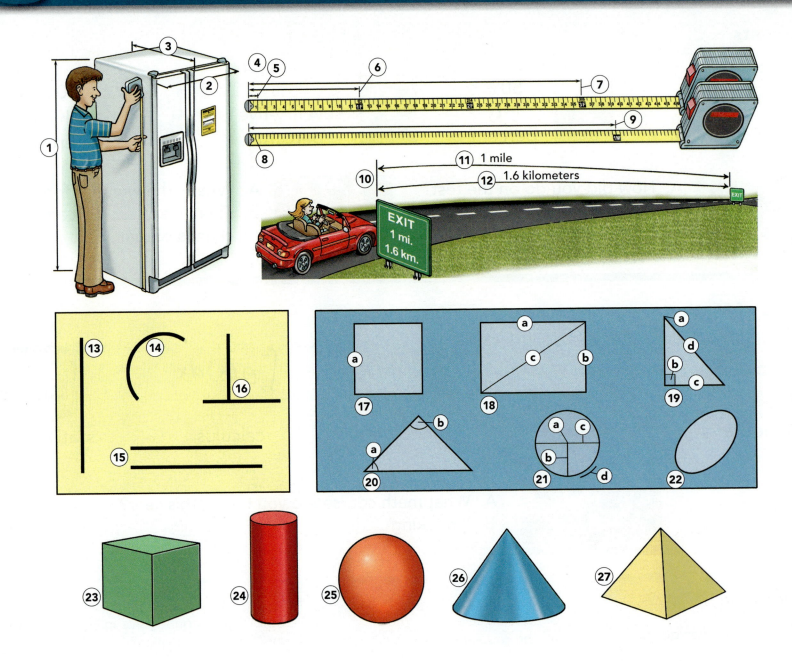

1 mile

1.6 kilometers

EXIT
1 mi.
1.6 km.

Measurements

1 height
2 width
3 depth
4 length
5 inch
6 foot–feet
7 yard
8 centimeter
9 meter
10 distance
11 mile
12 kilometer

Lines

13 straight line
14 curved line
15 parallel lines
16 perpendicular lines

Geometric Shapes

17 square
  a side
18 rectangle
  a length
  b width
  c diagonal
19 right triangle
  a apex
  b right angle
  c base
  d hypotenuse
20 isosceles triangle
  a acute angle
  b obtuse angle
21 circle
  a center
  b radius
  c diameter
  d circumference
22 ellipse/oval

Solid Figures

23 cube
24 cylinder
25 sphere
26 cone
27 pyramid

[1–9]
A. What's the _____[1–4]____?
B. .... ____[5–9]____(s).

[11–12]
A. What's the distance?
B. .... _____(s).

1 inch (1") = 2.54 centimeters (cm)
1 foot (1') = 0.305 meters (m)
1 yard (1 yd.) = 0.914 meters (m)
1 mile (mi.) = 1.6 kilometers (km)

[17–22]
A. What shape is this?
B. It's a/an _____.

[23–27]
A. What figure is this?
B. It's a/an _____.

[13–27]
A. This painting is magnificent!
B. Hmm. I don't think so. It just looks like a lot of _____s and _____s to me!

Types of Sentences & Parts of Speech

A *Students study in the new library.*
①   ②   ③ ④   ⑤

C *Read page nine.*

B *Do they study hard?*
⑥   ⑦

D *This cake is fantastic!*

A declarative	**1** noun	**5** adjective
B interrogative	**2** verb	**6** pronoun
C imperative	**3** preposition	**7** adverb
D exclamatory	**4** article	

A. What type of sentence is this?
B. It's a/an __[A–D]__ sentence.

A. What part of speech is this?
B. It's a/an __[1–7]__ .

Punctuation Marks & the Writing Process

8 period
9 question mark
10 exclamation point
11 comma

12 apostrophe
13 quotation marks
14 colon
15 semi-colon

16 brainstorm ideas
17 organize *my* ideas
18 write a first draft
  a title
  b paragraph

19 make corrections/ revise/edit
20 get feedback
21 write a final copy/ rewrite

A. Did you find any mistakes?
B. Yes. You forgot to put a/an ___[8–15]___ in this sentence.

A. Are you working on your composition?
B. Yes. I'm ___[16–21]___ing.

1 fiction
2 novel
3 short story
4 poetry/poems
5 non-fiction

6 biography
7 autobiography
8 essay
9 report
10 magazine article

11 newspaper article
12 editorial
13 letter
14 postcard
15 note

16 invitation
17 thank-you note
18 memo
19 e-mail
20 instant message

A. What are you doing?
B. I'm writing $\begin{cases} \underline{\quad [1, 4, 5] \quad}. \\ \text{a/an} \ \underline{\quad [2, 3, 6–20] \quad}. \end{cases}$

What kind of literature do you like to read?
What are some of your favorite books?
Who is your favorite author?

Do you like to read
newspapers and magazines?
Which ones do you read?

Do you sometimes send or receive
letters, postcards, notes, e-mail, or
instant messages? Tell about the
people you communicate with,
and how.

1 forest / woods

2 hill

3 mountain range

4 mountain peak

5 valley

6 lake

7 plains

8 meadow

9 stream / brook

10 pond

11 plateau

12 canyon

13 dune / sand dune

14 desert

15 jungle

16 seashore / shore

17 bay

18 ocean

19 island

20 peninsula

21 rainforest

22 river

23 waterfall

A. { This is a beautiful _____!
These are beautiful _____s!

B. I agree. It's / They're magnificent!

Tell about the geography of your country. Describe the different geographic features.

Have you seen some of the geographic features in this lesson? Which ones? Where?

Science Equipment

1 microscope
2 computer
3 slide
4 Petri dish
5 flask
6 funnel

7 beaker
8 test tube
9 forceps
10 crucible tongs
11 Bunsen burner
12 graduated cylinder

13 magnet
14 prism
15 dropper
16 chemicals
17 balance
18 scale

The Scientific Method

A state the problem
B form a hypothesis
C plan a procedure
D do a procedure
E make/record observations
F draw conclusions

A. What do we need to do this procedure?
B. We need a/an/the __[1–18]__ .

A. How is your experiment coming along?
B. I'm getting ready to __[A–F]__ .

Do you have experience with the scientific equipment in this lesson? Tell about it.

What science courses do/did you take in school?

Think of an idea for a science experiment.
What question about science do you want to answer? State the problem.
What do you think will happen in the experiment? Form a hypothesis.
How can you test your hypothesis? Plan a procedure.

1 accountant	6 babysitter	10 businessman	15 chef/cook
2 actor	7 baker	11 businesswoman	16 child day-care worker
3 actress	8 barber	12 butcher	17 computer software engineer
4 artist	9 bricklayer/mason	13 carpenter	
5 assembler		14 cashier	18 construction worker

[1–5]
A. What do you do?
B. I'm an **accountant**.

[6–16]
A. What do you do?
B. I'm a **babysitter**.

Which of these occupations do you think is the most interesting?   Why?

1 custodian/janitor

2 data entry clerk

3 delivery person

4 dockworker

5 factory worker

6 farmer

7 firefighter

8 fisher

9 food-service worker

10 foreman

11 gardener/landscaper

12 garment worker

13 hairdresser

14 health-care aide/attendant

15 home health aide/home attendant

16 homemaker

A. What do you do?

B. I'm a **custodian**.

Which of these occupations do you think is the most difficult? Why?

1 housekeeper
2 lawyer
3 machine operator
4 mail carrier/letter carrier
5 manager
6 manicurist
7 mechanic
8 medical assistant/physician assistant

9 messenger/courier
10 mover
11 painter
12 pharmacist
13 photographer
14 pilot
15 police officer
16 receptionist

A. What's your occupation?
B. I'm a **housekeeper**.
A. A **housekeeper**?
B. Yes. That's right.

Which of these occupations do you think is the most important? Why?

1 repairperson
2 salesperson
3 sanitation worker/trash collector
4 secretary
5 security guard
6 serviceman
7 servicewoman
8 stock clerk
9 store owner/shopkeeper

10 supervisor
11 tailor
12 teacher/instructor
13 translator/interpreter
14 truck driver
15 veterinarian/vet
16 waiter/server
17 waitress/server
18 welder

A. What do you do?
B. I'm a **repairperson**. How about you?
A. I'm a **secretary**.

Do you work? What's your occupation? What are the occupations of the people in your family?

1 act
2 assemble *components*
3 assist *patients*
4 build *things*/construct *things*
5 clean
6 cook
7 deliver *pizzas*
8 draw

9 drive *a truck*
10 file
11 fly *an airplane*
12 grow *vegetables*
13 guard *buildings*
14 manage *a restaurant*
15 mow *lawns*
16 operate *equipment*

A. Can you **act**?
B. Yes, I can.

Can you do any of these activities? Which ones?

1 paint
2 prepare *food*
3 repair *things*/fix *things*
4 sell *cars*
5 serve *food*
6 sew
7 speak *Spanish*
8 supervise *people*

9 take care of *elderly people*
10 take inventory
11 teach
12 translate
13 type
14 use *a cash register*
15 wash *dishes*
16 write

A. Do you know how to **paint**?
B. Yes, I do.

Tell about your job skills. What can you do?

① HELP WANTED

② POSITION AVAILABLE

Position: Secretary
Location: Office of the Director
Date Available: Now
Skills Required: Typing, word processing, filing, phone skills
Application Deadline: Friday, January 8, 5 P.M.
Apply to: Ms. Tina Green, Personnel Department

Apply in person

CASHIERS

③ ⑥ ⑦
FT & PT positions avail. $11/hr.

④ ⑤
M-F. Days & eves. Prev. exper. req.
⑨ ⑩ ⑪ ⑫

⑧

Excel. salary. Save-Mart, 2540 Central Ave.
⑬

COOKS

Ⓐ Ⓑ Is the job still available?

Ⓒ I'd like to come in for an interview.

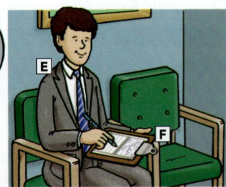

Ⓓ

Ⓔ Ⓕ

Ⓖ Ⓗ I can . . .

Ⓘ I worked at . . .

Ⓙ $$?

Ⓚ health care? sick days?

Ⓛ Dear Ms. Wilson, Thank you

Ⓜ You're hired!

Types of Job Ads

1 help wanted sign
2 job notice /
   job announcement
3 classified ad /
   want ad

Job Ad Abbreviations

4 full-time
5 part-time
6 available
7 hour
8 Monday through Friday
9 evenings
10 previous
11 experience
12 required
13 excellent

Job Search

A respond to an ad
B request information
C request an interview
D prepare a resume
E dress appropriately
F fill out an application (form)
G go to an interview
H talk about your skills and qualifications
I talk about your experience
J ask about the salary
K ask about the benefits
L write a thank-you note
M get hired

A. How did you find your job?
B. I found it through a ___[1–3]___ .

A. How was your job interview?
B. It went very well.
A. Did you ___[D–F, H–M]___?
B. Yes, I did.

Tell about a job you are familiar with. What are the skills and qualifications required for the job? What are the hours? What is the salary?

Tell about how people you know found their jobs.

Tell about your own experience with a job search or a job interview.

1 time clock
2 time cards
3 locker room
4 (assembly) line
5 (factory) worker
6 work station
7 line supervisor
8 quality control supervisor
9 machine
10 conveyor belt
11 warehouse
12 packer

13 forklift
14 freight elevator
15 union notice
16 suggestion box
17 shipping department
18 shipping clerk
19 hand truck / dolly
20 loading dock
21 payroll office
22 personnel office

A. Excuse me. I'm a new employee.
   Where's / Where are the _____?
B. Next to / Near / In / On the _____.

A. Where's *Tony*?
B. *He's* in / on / at / next to / near the _____.

Are there any factories where you live? What kind? What are the working conditions there?

What products do factories in your country produce?

1 sledgehammer
2 pickax
3 shovel
4 wheelbarrow
5 jackhammer/pneumatic drill
6 blueprints
7 ladder
8 tape measure
9 toolbelt
10 trowel
11 cement mixer

12 scaffolding
13 dump truck
14 front-end loader
15 crane
16 cherry picker
17 bulldozer
18 backhoe
19 concrete mixer truck
20 pickup truck
21 trailer

22 drywall
23 wood/lumber
24 plywood
25 insulation
26 wire
27 brick
28 shingle
29 pipe
30 girder/beam

A. Could you get me that/those __[1–10]__?
B. Sure.

A. Watch out for that __[11–21]__!
B. Oh! Thanks for the warning!

A. Do we have enough __[22–26]__ / __[27–30]__s?
B. I think so.

What building materials is your home made of?

Describe a construction site near your home or school.
Tell about the construction equipment and the materials.

1
2
3
4
5
6

7

8

9
10
11

12

13

14
15
16
17

18 DANGER

19 CAUTION HAZARDOUS AREA

20

21

22
23
24
25 EXIT
ALARM WILL SOUND

1 hard hat / helmet
2 earplugs
3 goggles
4 safety vest
5 safety boots
6 toe guard
7 back support

8 safety earmuffs
9 hairnet
10 mask
11 latex gloves
12 respirator
13 safety glasses

14 flammable
15 poisonous
16 corrosive
17 radioactive
18 dangerous
19 hazardous

20 biohazard
21 electrical hazard
22 first-aid kit
23 fire extinguisher
24 defibrillator
25 emergency exit

A. Don't forget to wear your ___[1–13]___ !
B. Thanks for reminding me.

A. Be careful! { That material is ___[14–17]___ !
That machine is ___[18]___ !
That work area is ___[19]___ !
That's a ___[20]___ ! / That's an ___[21]___ !
B. Thanks for the warning.

A. Where's the ___[22–25]___ ?
B. It's over there.

Do you / Did you ever use any of the safety equipment in this lesson? When? Where?

Where do you see safety equipment in your community?

A bus

1 bus stop
2 bus route
3 passenger
4 (bus) fare
5 transfer
6 bus driver
7 bus station
8 ticket counter
9 ticket
10 baggage compartment

B train

11 train station
12 ticket window
13 arrival and departure board
14 information booth
15 schedule/timetable
16 platform
17 track
18 conductor

C subway

19 subway station
20 (subway) token
21 turnstile
22 fare card
23 fare card machine

D taxi

24 taxi stand
25 taxi/cab
26 meter
27 cab driver/taxi driver

E ferry

[A–E]
A. How are you going to get there?
B. { I'm going to take the ___[A–C, E]___ .
     I'm going to take a ___[D]___ .

[1, 7, 8, 10–19, 21, 23–25]
A. Excuse me. Where's the _____?
B. Over there.

How do you get to different places in your community?
Describe public transportation where you live.

In your country, can you travel far by train or by bus?
Where can you go? How much do tickets cost?
Describe the buses and trains.

PREPOSITIONS OF MOTION

1 over the bridge
2 under the bridge
3 through the tunnel
4 around the corner

5 up the street
6 down the street
7 across the street
8 past the *school*

9 on
10 off
11 into
12 out of
13 onto

[1–8]
A. Go **over** the bridge.
B. **Over** the bridge?
A. Yes.

[9–13]
A. I can't talk right now. I'm getting **on** a train.
B. You're getting **on** a train?
A. Yes. I'll call you later.

What places do you go past on your way to school?

Tell how to get to different places from your home or your school.

Traffic Signs

1 stop
2 no left turn
3 no right turn
4 no U-turn
5 right turn only
6 do not enter
7 one way
8 dead end/no outlet
9 pedestrian crossing
10 railroad crossing
11 school crossing
12 merging traffic
13 yield
14 detour
15 slippery when wet
16 handicapped parking only

Compass Directions

17 north
18 south
19 west
20 east

Road Test Instructions

21 Turn left.
22 Turn right.
23 Go straight.
24 Parallel park.
25 Make a 3-point turn.
26 Use hand signals.

[1–16]
A. Careful! That sign says "**stop**"!
B. Oh. Thanks.

[17–20]
A. Which way should I go?
B. Go **north**.

[21–26]
A. Turn **right**.
B. Turn **right**?
A. Yes.

Which of these traffic signs are in your neighborhood? What other traffic signs do you usually see?

Describe any differences between traffic signs in different countries you know.

A Check-In

1 ticket
2 ticket counter
3 ticket agent
4 suitcase
5 arrival and departure monitor

B Security

6 security checkpoint
7 metal detector
8 security officer
9 X-ray machine
10 carry-on bag

C The Gate

11 check-in counter
12 boarding pass
13 gate
14 boarding area

D Baggage Claim

15 baggage claim (area)
16 baggage
17 luggage carrier
18 garment bag
19 baggage claim check

E Customs and Immigration

20 customs
21 customs officer
22 customs declaration form
23 immigration
24 immigration officer
25 passport
26 visa

[2, 3, 5–9, 11, 13–15, 20, 21, 23, 24]
A. Excuse me. Where's the _____?*
B. Right over there.

*With 20 and 23 use: Excuse me. Where's _____?

[1, 4, 10, 12, 16–19, 22, 25, 26]
A. Oh, no! I can't find my _____!
B. I'll help you look for it.

Describe an airport you are familiar with. Tell about the check-in area, the security area, the gates, and the baggage claim area.

Tell about a time you went through Customs and Immigration.

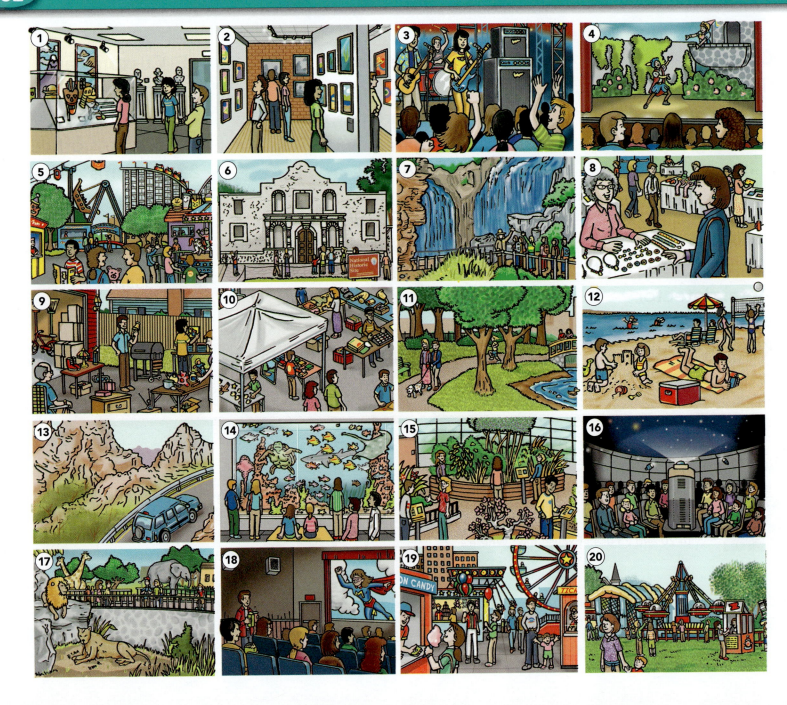

1 museum
2 art gallery
3 concert
4 play
5 amusement park
6 historic site
7 national park
8 craft fair
9 yard sale
10 swap meet/flea market

11 park
12 beach
13 mountains
14 aquarium
15 botanical gardens
16 planetarium
17 zoo
18 movies
19 carnival
20 fair

A. What do you want to do today?

B. Let's go to $\begin{cases} \text{a/an} \underline{\quad[1-9]\quad}. \\ \text{the} \underline{\quad[10-20]\quad}. \end{cases}$

A. What did you do over the weekend?

B. I went to $\begin{cases} \text{a/an} \underline{\quad[1-9]\quad}. \\ \text{the} \underline{\quad[10-20]\quad}. \end{cases}$

A. What are you going to do on your day off?

B. I'm going to go to $\begin{cases} \text{a/an} \underline{\quad[1-9]\quad}. \\ \text{the} \underline{\quad[10-20]\quad}. \end{cases}$

What are some of your favorite places to go? Where are they? What do you do there?

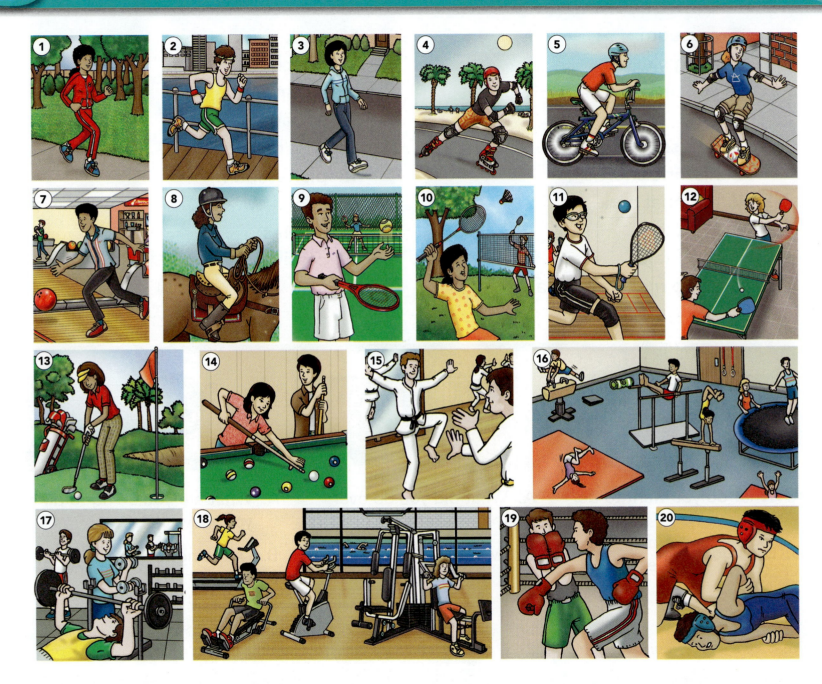

1 jogging
2 running
3 walking
4 inline skating/rollerblading
5 cycling/biking
6 skateboarding
7 bowling

8 horseback riding
9 tennis
10 badminton
11 racquetball
12 table tennis/ping pong
13 golf
14 billiards/pool

15 martial arts
16 gymnastics
17 weightlifting
18 work out/exercise
19 box
20 wrestle

[1–8]
A. What do you like to do in your free time?
B. I like to go **jogging**.

[9–14]
A. What do you like to do on the weekend?
B. I like to play **tennis**.

[15–17]
A. What do you like to do for exercise?
B. I like to do **martial arts**.

[18–20]
A. Do you exercise regularly?
B. Yes. I **work out** three times a week.

Do you do any of these activities? Which ones?

Which of these activities are popular in your country?

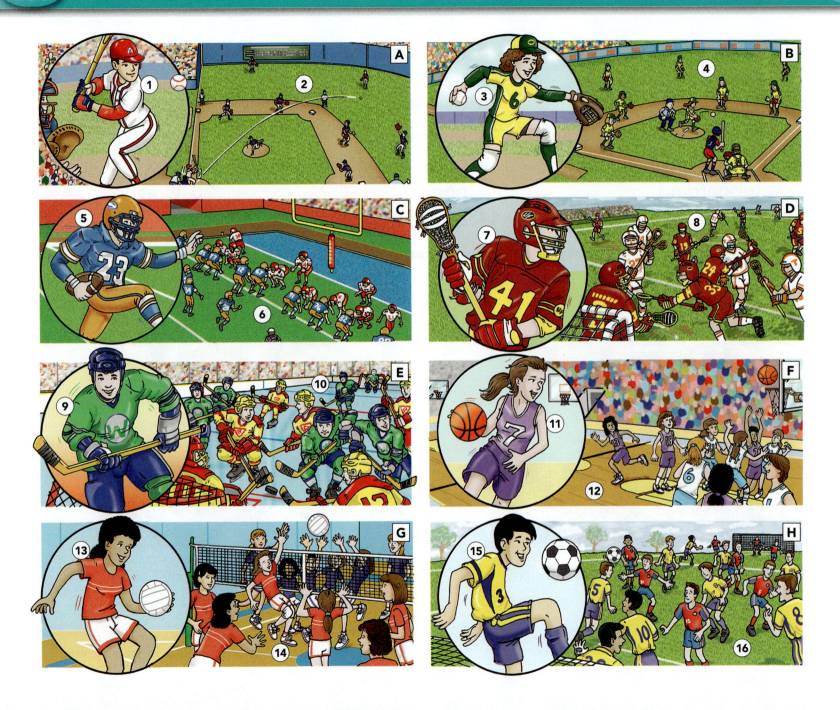

A baseball
1 baseball player
2 baseball field / ballfield

B softball
3 softball player
4 ballfield

C football
5 football player
6 football field

D lacrosse
7 lacrosse player
8 lacrosse field

E (ice) hockey
9 hockey player
10 hockey rink

F basketball
11 basketball player
12 basketball court

G volleyball
13 volleyball player
14 volleyball court

H soccer
15 soccer player
16 soccer field

[A–H]
A. Do you like to play **baseball**?
B. Yes. **Baseball** is one of my favorite sports.

A. .... plays __[A–H]__ very well.
B. You're right. I think he's/she's the best _____* on the team.

*Use 1, 3, 5, 7, 9, 11, 13, 15.

A. Now listen, team! Go out on that _____† and play the best game of __[A–H]__ you can!
B. All right, Coach!

† Use 2, 4, 6, 8, 10, 12, 14, 16.

Which sports in this lesson do you like to play? Which do you like to watch?

What are your favorite teams?

Name some famous players of these sports.

1 play	**music**	**movies/films**	**TV programs**
2 concert	**9** classical music	**15** drama	**20** game show/quiz show
3 music club	**10** popular music	**16** comedy	**21** talk show
4 dance club	**11** country music	**17** cartoon	**22** drama
5 comedy club	**12** rock music	**18** action movie/	**23** (situation) comedy/
6 movies	**13** jazz	adventure movie	sitcom
7 ballet	**14** hip hop	**19** horror movie	**24** children's program
8 opera			**25** news program

[1–8]

A. What are you doing this evening?

B. I'm going to { a ___[1–5]___ .
the ___[6–8]___ .

[9–14]

A. What kind of music do you like?

B. I like **classical music**.

[15–19]

A. What kind of movies do you like?

B. I like **drama**s.

[20–25]

A. What kind of TV programs do you like to watch?

B. I like to watch **talk show**s.

What kinds of entertainment in this lesson do you like?
What kinds of entertainment are popular in your country?

What's your favorite type of music? Who is your favorite singer? musician? musical group?

What kind of movies do you like?
Who are you favorite movie stars?
What are the titles of your favorite movies?

What kind of TV programs do you like?
What are your favorite shows?

1

Florida *the Sunshine State*
DRIVER LICENSE CLASS D
D200-555-44-111-0
Dawn Erics
220 Palisades Way
Miami, FL 33017-0000
DOB: 05-20-65   SEX: F   HGT: 5-07
ISSUED: 05-19-05
EXPIRES: 05-20-11
REST BF
ENDORSE
Dawn Erics
ORGAN DONOR
Q123456789000   SAFE DRIVER
Operation of a motor vehicle constitutes consent to any sobriety test required by law.

2

SOCIAL SECURITY
142-84-5194
THIS NUMBER HAS BEEN ESTABLISHED FOR
PATRICK MICHAEL GAFFNEY
Patrick Michael Gaffney
SIGNATURE

3

International *Student* Identit Card
Carte d'étudiant internationale / Carné internacional de estudiante
STUDENT
Studies at / Étudiant à / Est. de Enseñanza
School of Audio Engineering
Name / Nom / Nombre
Robert Oliver
Born /Né(e) le / Nacido/a el
19 FEB 1986
Validity / Validité / Validez
09/2005 - 12/2006
ISIC
S 044 201 440 365

4

Global Computer
Dawn Erics
Associate Sales Manager
ID# 752-775-754-752

5

PERMANENT RESIDENT CARD
NAME   RIVERA, CARLOS M.
INS A#   A92475816
Birthdate   Category   Sex
03/17/66   IR6   M
Country of Birth
Mexico
CARD EXPIRES   06/29/09
Resident Since   11/17/99
C1USA0924758166EAC0013440673<<
6003029M1004268MEX<<<<<<<<<<0
RIVERA<<CARLOS<<<<<<<<<<<<<<<

6

PASSPORT
United States of America

7

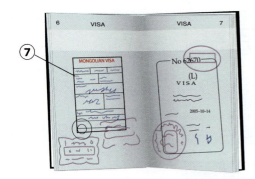

6   VISA   VISA   7
MONGOLIAN VISA
No 62670
(L)
VISA
2005-10-14

8

WORK PERMIT

INDIVIDUAL WORK PERMIT:
1. Employer completes and signs
2. Parent or guardian completes and signs
3. Employer submits work permit and LEGIBLE copy of minor's proof of age to the Wage and Hour office.
4. When the approved work permit is returned, the minor may begin work.

GENERAL DUTIES WORK PERMIT:
1. Employer completes and signs
2. Employer submits work permit to Wage and Hour office.
3. The approved duties are returned to the employer. After employer obtains the signature of the minor's parent or guardian then the minor may begin work.
4. Employer must return a copy of the work permit signed by the parent or legal guardian and LEGIBLE copy of proof of age to the Wage and Hour office within seven (7) calendar days of minor beginning work.

☐ INDIVIDUAL WORK PERMIT
☐ GENERAL DUTIES WORK PERMIT APPROVED FOR:
☐ 16 & 17 YEAR OLDS; OR
☐ 14 - 17 YEAR OLDS
☐ APPROVED AS AMENDED
☐ DISAPPROVED

By:_____
Date:_____

Return permit to employer's FAX number:
_____

Section (A) to be completed by EMPLOYER

Name of Employer: DBA/

Employer's Local Mailing Address: City: Zip

9

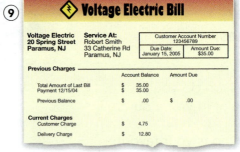

⚡ Voltage Electric Bill

Voltage Electric
20 Spring Street
Paramus, NJ

Service At:
Robert Smith
33 Catherine Rd
Paramus, NJ

Customer Account Number
123456789
Due Date: Amount Due:
January 15, 2005 $35.00

Previous Charges

	Account Balance	Amount Due
Total Amount of Last Bill	$ 35.00	
Payment 12/15/04	$ 35.00	
Previous Balance	$ .00	$ .00

Current Charges

Customer Charge	$	4.75
Delivery Charge	$	12.80

10

CERTIFICATE OF BIRTH
(In the Clerks office of the County Commision of Randolf County)

I, MARK PALMER, Clerk of the County Commision in the County and State aforesaid, it being an office of record, and having a seal, do hereby certify that the records in my office show that

Was born at _____ Sex _____
of New Jersey on the _____ day of _____ in Bergen County and the State and that the parents names are as follows:
Father's name
Mother's maiden name
are recorded in Birth Record No. _____ at page _____ Date filed: _____

In testimony whereof, I have hereunto affixed my signature and official seal at Bergen County, NJ this _____ day of _____, 20 ____, _____, Clerk

1 driver's license
2 social security card
3 student I.D. card
4 employee I.D. badge

5 permanent resident card
6 passport
7 visa

8 work permit
9 proof of residence
10 birth certificate

A. May I see your _____?
B. Yes. Here you are.

A. Oh, no! I can't find my _____!
B. I'll help you look for it.
A. Thanks.

Which forms of identification do you have? When do you need to show them?

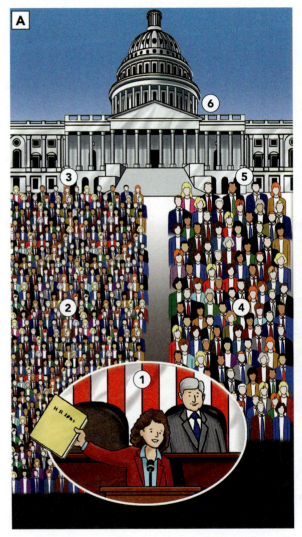

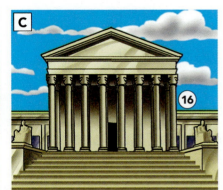

A legislative branch

1 makes the laws
2 representatives /
   congressmen and
   congresswomen
3 house of representatives
4 senators
5 senate
6 Capitol Building

B executive branch

7 enforces the laws
8 president
9 vice-president
10 cabinet
11 White House

C judicial branch

12 explains the laws
13 Supreme Court justices
14 chief justice
15 Supreme Court
16 Supreme Court Building

A. Which branch of government [1, 7, 12] ?
B. The [A, B, C] .

A. Who works in the [A, B, C] of the government?
B. The [2, 4, 8–10, 13, 14] .

A. Where do/does the [2, 4, 8–10, 13, 14] work?
B. In the [6, 11, 16] .

A. In which branch of the government is the [3, 5, 10, 15] ?
B. In the [A, B, C] .

Compare the governments of different countries you are familiar with. What are the
branches of government? Who works there? What do they do?

A The Constitution
1 "the supreme law of the land"
2 the Preamble

B The Bill of Rights
3 the first 10 amendments to the Constitution

C The 1st Amendment
4 freedom of speech
5 freedom of the press
6 freedom of religion
7 freedom of assembly

D Other Amendments
8 ended slavery
9 gave African-Americans the right to vote
10 established income taxes
11 gave women the right to vote
12 gave citizens eighteen years and older the right to vote

A. What is __[A ,B]__ ?
B. __[1 ,3]__ .

A. Which amendment guarantees people __[4–7]__ ?
B. The 1st Amendment.

A. Which amendment __[8–12]__ ?
B. The _____ Amendment.

A. What did the _____ Amendment do?
B. It __[8–12]__ .

Describe how people in your community exercise their 1st Amendment rights. What are some examples of freedom of speech? the press? religion? assembly?

Do you have an idea for a new amendment? Tell about it and why you think it's important.

1 New Year's Day
2 Martin Luther King, Jr.* Day
3 Valentine's Day
4 Memorial Day

* Jr. = Junior

5 Independence Day /
  the Fourth of July
6 Halloween
7 Veterans Day
8 Thanksgiving

9 Christmas
10 Ramadan
11 Kwanzaa
12 Hanukkah

A. When is ___[1, 3, 5, 6, 7, 9]___ ?
B. It's on ...(date)... .

A. When is ___[2, 4, 8]___ ?
B. It's in ...(month)... .

A. When does ___[10–12]___
   begin this year?
B. It begins on ...(date)... .

Which of these holidays do you celebrate? How?   What holidays do people celebrate in your country?

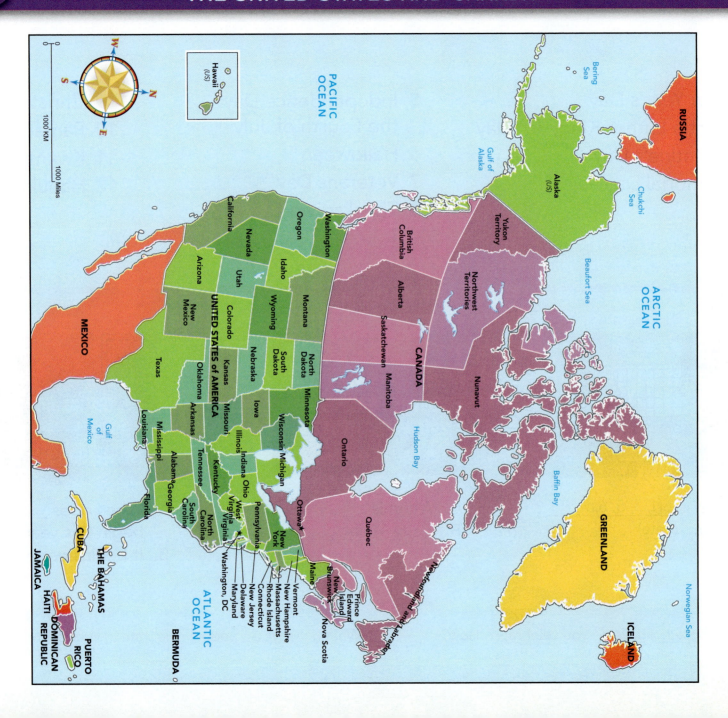

PACIFIC OCEAN

Hawaii (US)

1000 KM

1000 Miles

California

Oregon

Washington

Nevada

Arizona

Idaho

Utah

New Mexico

Colorado

Wyoming

Montana

UNITED STATES of AMERICA

Texas

Oklahoma

Kansas

Nebraska

South Dakota

North Dakota

Minnesota

MEXICO

Gulf of Mexico

Louisiana

Arkansas

Missouri

Iowa

Wisconsin

Michigan

Mississippi

Alabama

Tennessee

Kentucky

Illinois

Indiana

Ohio

Georgia

Florida

South Carolina

North Carolina

West Virginia

Virginia

Pennsylvania

New York

Washington, DC

Maryland

Delaware

New Jersey

Connecticut

Rhode Island

Massachusetts

New Hampshire

Vermont

Maine

British Columbia

Alberta

Saskatchewan

Manitoba

Yukon Territory

Northwest Territories

Nunavut

CANADA

Ontario

Québec

New Brunswick

Prince Edward Island

Nova Scotia

Newfoundland and Labrador

Alaska (US)

Gulf of Alaska

Bering Sea

Chukchi Sea

Beaufort Sea

RUSSIA

ARCTIC OCEAN

Hudson Bay

Baffin Bay

GREENLAND

Norwegian Sea

Ottawa

CUBA

THE BAHAMAS

JAMAICA

HAITI

DOMINICAN REPUBLIC

PUERTO RICO

BERMUDA

ATLANTIC OCEAN

ICELAND

N
S
E
W

UNITED STATES of AMERICA

BAJA CALIFORNIA

SONORA

CHIHUAHUA

COAHUILA

Gulf of California

BAJA CALIFORNIA SUR

MEXICO

DURANGO

NUEVO LEÓN

SINALOA

ZACATECAS

TAMAULIPAS

PACIFIC OCEAN

NAYARIT

SAN LUIS POTOSÍ

AGUASCALIENTES

QUERÉTARO

HIDALGO

DISTRITO FEDERAL

JALISCO

TLAXCALA

GUANAJUATO

VERACRUZ

COLIMA

Mexico City

MICHOACÁN

PUEBLA

MÉXICO

MORELOS

GUERRERO

OAXACA

YUCATÁN

QUINTANA ROO

CAMPECHE

TABASCO

CHIAPAS

Gulf of Tehuantepec

GUATEMALA

Guatemala City

San Salvador

EL SALVADOR

BELIZE

Belmopan

HONDURAS

Tegucigalpa

NICARAGUA

Managua

COSTA RICA

San José

Panama City

PANAMA

Gulf of Mexico

Havana

CUBA

THE BAHAMAS

Nassau

TURKS AND CAICOS ISLANDS

ATLANTIC OCEAN

CAYMAN ISLANDS

JAMAICA

Kingston

Port-au-Prince

HAITI

DOMINICAN REPUBLIC

Santo Domingo

PUERTO RICO

San Juan

VIRGIN ISLANDS (US & UK)

ANGUILLA

SAINT KITTS AND NEVIS

ANTIGUA AND BARBUDA

MONTSERRAT

GUADELOUPE

DOMINICA

MARTINIQUE

BARBADOS

SAINT LUCIA

SAINT VINCENT AND THE GRENADINES

GRENADA

Caribbean Sea

NETHERLANDS ANTILLES

ARUBA

Port of Spain

TRINIDAD AND TOBAGO

Caracas

COLOMBIA

VENEZUELA

N

W E

S

0   500 Miles

0   500 KM

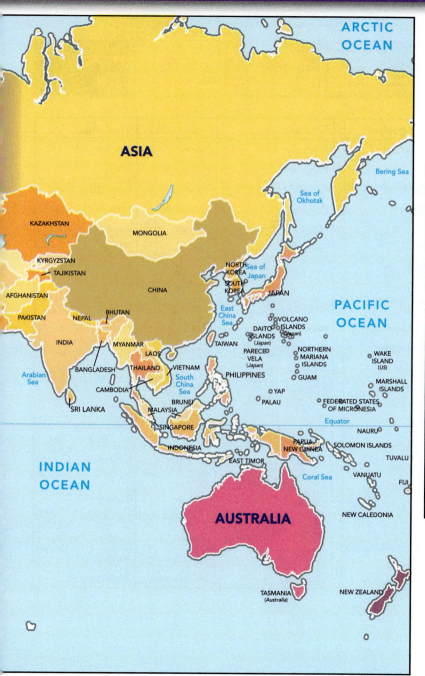

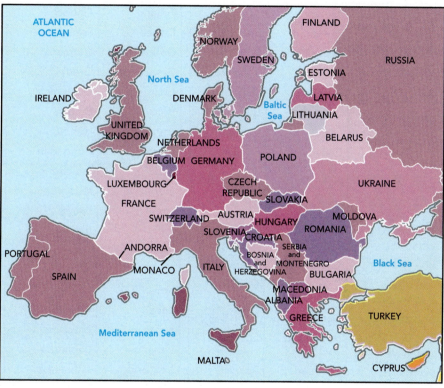

Country	Nationality	Language
Afghanistan	Afghan	Afghan
Argentina	Argentine	Spanish
Australia	Australian	English
Bolivia	Bolivian	Spanish
Brazil	Brazilian	Portuguese
Bulgaria	Bulgarian	Bulgarian
Cambodia	Cambodian	Cambodian
Canada	Canadian	English/ French
Chile	Chilean	Spanish
China	Chinese	Chinese
Colombia	Colombian	Spanish
Costa Rica	Costa Rican	Spanish
Cuba	Cuban	Spanish
(The) Czech Republic	Czech	Czech
Denmark	Danish	Danish
(The) Dominican Republic	Dominican	Spanish
Ecuador	Ecuadorian	Spanish
Egypt	Egyptian	Arabic
El Salvador	Salvadorean	Spanish
England	English	English
Estonia	Estonian	Estonian
Ethiopia	Ethiopian	Amharic

Country	Nationality	Language
Finland	Finnish	Finnish
France	French	French
Germany	German	German
Greece	Greek	Greek
Guatemala	Guatemalan	Spanish
Haiti	Haitian	Haitian Kreyol
Honduras	Honduran	Spanish
Hungary	Hungarian	Hungarian
India	Indian	Hindi
Indonesia	Indonesian	Indonesian
Israel	Israeli	Hebrew
Italy	Italian	Italian
Japan	Japanese	Japanese
Jordan	Jordanian	Arabic
Korea	Korean	Korean
Laos	Laotian	Laotian
Latvia	Latvian	Latvian
Lebanon	Lebanese	Arabic
Lithuania	Lithuanian	Lithuanian
Malaysia	Malaysian	Malay
Mexico	Mexican	Spanish
New Zealand	New Zealander	English
Nicaragua	Nicaraguan	Spanish

Country	Nationality	Language
Norway	Norwegian	Norwegian
Pakistan	Pakistani	Urdu
Panama	Panamanian	Spanish
Peru	Peruvian	Spanish
(The) Philippines	Filipino	Tagalog
Poland	Polish	Polish
Portugal	Portuguese	Portuguese
Puerto Rico	Puerto Rican	Spanish
Romania	Romanian	Romanian
Russia	Russian	Russian
Saudi Arabia	Saudi	Arabic
Slovakia	Slovak	Slovak
Spain	Spanish	Spanish
Sweden	Swedish	Swedish
Switzerland	Swiss	German/French/ Italian
Taiwan	Taiwanese	Chinese
Thailand	Thai	Thai
Turkey	Turkish	Turkish
Ukraine	Ukrainian	Ukrainian
(The) United States	American	English
Venezuela	Venezuelan	Spanish
Vietnam	Vietnamese	Vietnamese

Regular Verbs

Regular verbs have four different spelling patterns for the past and past participle forms.

1 Add **–ed** to the end of the verb. For example: act → act**ed**

act	burp	deliver	floss	lower	pour	saute	talk
add	cash	discuss	form	mark	print	scratch	turn
answer	check	dress	grill	match	record	seat	twist
ask	clean	drill	guard	mix	relax	select	vacuum
assist	clear	dust	hand (in)	mow	repair	shorten	vomit
bank	collect	edit	help	open	repeat	sign	walk
boil	comb	end	insert	paint	request	simmer	wash
box	construct	enter	iron	pass (out)	respond	spell	watch
brainstorm	cook	establish	leak	peel	rest	sprain	wax
broil	correct	explain	lengthen	plant	return	steam	work
brush	cough	faint	listen	play	roast	swallow	
burn	cross (out)	fix	look	polish	rock		

2 Add **–d** to a verb that ends in **–e**. For example: assemble → assemble**d**

assemble	change	erase	introduce	operate	raise	shave	type
bake	circle	examine	manage	organize	remove	slice	underline
balance	close	exchange	measure	overdose	revise	sneeze	unscramble
barbecue	combine	exercise	microwave	practice	scrape	state	use
bathe	describe	file	move	prepare	serve	supervise	wheeze
bruise	dislocate	gargle	nurse	pronounce	share	translate	wrestle
bubble	enforce	grate					

3 Double the final consonant and add **–ed** to the end of the verb. For example: chop → chop**ped**

chop	plan	transfer
mop	stir	

4 Drop the final **–y** and add **–ied** to the end of the verb. For example: apply → appl**ied**

apply	dry	stir-fry	try
copy	fry	study	

Irregular Verbs

The following verbs have irregular past tense and/or past participle forms.

be	was	were		leave	left	left
beat	beat	beaten		let	let	let
bleed	bled	bled		make	made	made
break	broke	broken		meet	met	met
bring	brought	brought		pay	paid	paid
build	built	built		put	put	put
buy	bought	bought		read	read	read
choose	chose	chosen		rewrite	rewrote	rewritten
come	came	come		ring	rang	rung
cut	cut	cut		say	said	said
do	did	done		see	saw	seen
draw	drew	drawn		sell	sold	sold
drink	drank	drunk		set	set	set
drive	drove	driven		sit	sat	sat
eat	ate	eaten		sleep	slept	slept
fall	fell	fallen		speak	spoke	spoken
feed	fed	fed		stand	stood	stood
fly	flew	flown		sweep	swept	swept
get	got	gotten		swim	swam	swum
give	gave	given		take	took	taken
go	went	gone		teach	taught	taught
grow	grew	grown		throw	threw	thrown
have	had	had		understand	understood	understood
hold	held	held		withdraw	withdrew	withdrawn
hurt	hurt	hurt		write	wrote	written

The bold number indicates the page(s) on which the word appears. The number that follows indicates the word's location in the illustration and in the word list on the page. For example, "address 3-5" indicates that the word address is on page 3 and is item number 5.

35 millimeter camera **149**-28
A.M. **37**
A.V. crew **191**-12
abdomen **163**-22
above **19**-1
accountant **205**-1
Ace™ bandage **171**-10
acorn squash **99**-13
across the street **227**-7
act **213**-1
action movie **239**-18
activities director **161**-12
actor **205**-2
actress **205**-3
acupuncture **179**-8
acute angle **195**-20a
ad **217**-A
add **117**-10
addition **192**
address **3**-5
adhesive tape **171**-8
adjective **196**-5
adult **85**-7
adventure movie **239**-18
adverb **196**-7
afraid **95**-11
African-American **245**-9
afternoon **43**-5
age **85**
AIDS **173**-25
air conditioner **61**-28
air conditioning **67**-10
air freshener **57**-22
air letter **157**-3
air purifier **179**-11
aisle **111**-1
alarm clock **51**-15
alcohol **177**-10

algebra **193**
allergic reaction **173**-7
aluminum foil **109**-12
ambulance **161**-8
amendment **245**-3,D
American cheese **105**-8
ammonia **69**-14
amusement park **233**-5
anesthesiologist **183**-17
anesthetic **177**-F
angry **95**-1
ankle **165**-11
anniversary **41**-27
annoyed **93**-16
answer the question
    13-19, **17**-8
answering machine
    149-26
antacid tablets **181**-8
antibiotic ointment **171**-6
antipasto **127**-10
antipasto plate **127**-10
ants **65**-11c
apartment ads **61**-1
apartment building **45**-1
apartment listings **61**-2
apartment number **3**-8
apex **195**-19a
apostrophe **197**-12
apple **97**-1
apple juice **103**-15
apple pie **127**-25
appliance repairperson
    65-E
application form **217**-F
apply for a loan **153**-F
appointment **41**-28
apricot **97**-7
April **41**-16

aquarium **233**-14
area code **3**-12
arithmetic **192**
arm **163**-25
armchair **47**-29
around the corner **227**-4
arrival and departure
    board **225**-13
arrival and departure
    monitor **231**-5
art **189**-19
art gallery **233**-2
arteries **165**-30
artichoke **99**-27
article **196**-4
artist **205**-4
ask a question **13**-17
ask about the
    benefits **217**-K
ask about the salary
    217-J
ask *you* some questions
    about your health **175**-E
asparagus **99**-7
aspirin **171**-11, **181**-1
assemble **213**-2
assembler **205**-5
assembly line **219**-4
assist **213**-3
assistant principal **21**-6
asthma **173**-18
athletic supporter **135**-10
atlas **159**-24
ATM **153**-12
ATM card **153**-6
ATM machine **153**-12
attendant **207**-14
audiotape **149**-14, **159**-13
auditorium **21**-K

August **41**-20
aunt **7**-2
autobiography **199**-7
autumn **43**-29
available **217**-6
average height **85**-15
average weight **85**-18
avocado **97**-14

baby **5**-7, **85**-2
baby backpack **55**-29
baby carriage **55**-19
baby carrier **55**-21
baby cereal **109**-15
baby food **109**-16, **187**-1
baby frontpack **55**-28
baby lotion **187**-16
baby monitor **55**-2
baby powder **187**-11
baby products **109**
baby seat **55**-24
baby shampoo **187**-14
baby wipes **187**-10
babysitter **205**-6
back **163**-24
back door **59**-19
back support **223**-7
backache **167**-5
backhoe **221**-18
backpack **139**-24
backyard **59**
bacon **101**-11, **121**-11
bacon, lettuce, and
    tomato sandwich
    121-24
bad **89**-32
badminton **235**-10
bag **113**-1
bagel **121**-3

baggage **231**-16
baggage claim **231**-D,15
baggage claim area
    231-15
baggage claim
    check **231**-19
baggage compartment
    225-10
bagger **111**-11
baggy **143**-4
bake **117**-15
baked chicken **127**-14
baked goods **107**
baked potato **127**-18
baker **205**-7
bakery **73**-1
baking products **107**
balance **203**-17
balance the
    checkbook **155**-16
balcony **61**-21
bald **87**-12
ballet **239**-7
ballfield **237**-2,4
banana **97**-4
band **191**-1
bandage **171**-3
Band-Aid™ **171**-3
bank **73**-2
bank officer **153**-13
bank online **155**-18
bank vault **153**-8
bankbook **153**-5
barbecue **59**-22, **117**-23
barber **205**-8
barber shop **73**-3
barrette **139**-12
base **195**-19c
baseball **237**-A

hairdresser 207-13
hairnet 223-9
half 115, 192
half dollar 38-5
half past 36
half-gallon 113-19
halibut 101-20
Halloween 247-6
hallway 21-F, 63
ham 101-10, 105-4
ham and cheese
 sandwich 121-23
hamburger 119-1
hammer 71-1
hamper 57-15
hand 165-1
hand in your
 homework 15-5
hand truck 219-19
hand vacuum 69-8
handbag 139-21
handicapped parking
 only 229-16
handkerchief 139-16
handsome 91-17
handyman 67-D
Hanukkah 247-12
happy 93-10
hard 91-2,4
hard hat 223-1
hardware store 77-1
has no pulse 171-13a
hat 133-3
have breakfast 23-18
have dinner 23-20
have lunch 23-19
hazardous 223-19
hazy 33-4
head 113-9, 163-1
headache 167-1
headboard 51-2
headphones 149-20

health 175-E, 189-10
health club 77-2
health-care aide 207-14
hearing impaired 85-23
heart 165-18, 175-G
heart attack 173-6
heart disease 173-22
heat wave 33-18
heating and air
 conditioning service
 67-F
heating bill 155-11
heating pad 179-9
heating system 67-9
heatstroke 173-4
heavy 85-17, 89-13,15,
 143-11
heel 137-14, 165-12
height 85, 175-A, 195-1
Heimlich maneuver
 171-15
helmet 223-1
help each other 15-8
help wanted sign 217-1
herbal tea 103-28
hiccups 167-20
high 89-27, 143-7
high blood pressure
 173-23
high chair 55-25, 123-6
high heels 137-14
high-top sneakers 137-18
high-tops 137-18
hill 201-2
hip 163-28
hip hop 239-14
historic site 233-6
history 189-3
hockey 237-E
hockey player 237-9
hockey rink 237-10
hold 187-D

home attendant 207-15
home economics 189-14
home health aide 207-15
home repairperson 67-D
homemaker 207-16
homesick 95-8
honest 91-35
honeydew melon 97-16
horror movie 239-19
horseback riding 235-8
hose 71-17
hospital 77-3, 161-C
hospital bed 183-3
hospital gown 183-2
host 123-2
hostess 123-1
hot 33-22, 89-33, 93-5
hot chocolate 121-18
hot chocolate mix 103-29
hot dog 119-3
hot water heater 65-3
hotel 77-4
hour 217-7
house 45-2
house of representatives
 243-3
house painter 65-C
houseboat 45-12
Household Appliances
 Department 145-12
household bills 155
household items 109
housekeeper 209-1
Housewares
 Department 145-10
humid 33-8
humidifier 179-10
hungry 93-7
hurt 169-18, 173-1
husband 5-1
hydrogen peroxide 171-5
hygienist 177-21

hypertension 173-23
hypotenuse 195-19d
hypothesis 203-B

I.V. 183-6
ice cream 105-13, 119-14,
 127-26
ice cream shop 77-5
ice cream sundae 127-29
ice cream truck 83-7
ice hockey 237-E
ice pack 177-16
iced tea 121-16
ill 93-4
immigration 231-23
immigration officer
 231-24
imperative 196-C
in 19-10
in front of 19-3
in shock 173-2
inch 195-5
income tax 245-10
Independence Day 247-5
industrial arts 189-15
inexpensive 91-26
infant 85-2
infection 167-10
influenza 173-12
information 217-B
information booth 225-14
injection 177-14
injured 173-1
inline skating 235-4
insect bite 167-12
insect spray 71-25
insert the ATM card
 155-22
instant coffee 103-26
instant message 199-20
instructor 211-12
insulation 221-25

insurance card 177-3
intercom 55-2, 63-1
international club 191-15
interpreter 211-13
interrogative 196-B
intersection 83-3
interview 217-C,G
into 227-11
invitation 199-16
iron 25-4
is bleeding 171-17e
is choking 171-15c
island 201-19
isn't breathing 171-14b
isosceles triangle 195-20
itchy 169-24

jacket 131-10, 133-4,
 143-23
jackhammer 221-5
jail 81-12
jalapeño 99-33
jalapeño pepper 99-33
jam 107-12
janitor 207-1
January 41-13
jar 113-10
jaw 163-12
jazz 239-13
jealous 95-15
jeans 131-6
jello 127-27
jelly 107-13
jersey 131-7
jewelry box 51-19
Jewelry Counter 145-2
job ad abbreviations 217
job ads 217
job announcement 217-2
job notice 217-2
job search 217
jockstrap 135-10

Expressions

Cardinal Numbers

1	one
2	two
3	three
4	four
5	five
6	six
7	seven
8	eight
9	nine
10	ten
11	eleven
12	twelve
13	thirteen
14	fourteen
15	fifteen
16	sixteen
17	seventeen
18	eighteen
19	nineteen
20	twenty
21	twenty-one
22	twenty-two
30	thirty
40	forty
50	fifty
60	sixty
70	seventy
80	eighty
90	ninety
100	one hundred
101	one hundred (and) one
102	one hundred (and) two
1,000	one thousand
10,000	ten thousand
100,000	one hundred thousand
1,000,000	one million
1,000,000,000	one billion

Ordinal Numbers

1st	first
2nd	second
3rd	third
4th	fourth
5th	fifth
6th	sixth
7th	seventh
8th	eighth
9th	ninth
10th	tenth
11th	eleventh
12th	twelfth
13th	thirteenth
14th	fourteenth
15th	fifteenth
16th	sixteenth
17th	seventeenth
18th	eighteenth
19th	nineteenth
20th	twentieth
21st	twenty-first
22nd	twenty-second
30th	thirtieth
40th	fortieth
50th	fiftieth
60th	sixtieth
70th	seventieth
80th	eightieth
90th	ninetieth
100th	one hundredth
101st	one hundred (and) first
102nd	one hundred (and) second
1,000th	one thousandth
10,000th	ten thousandth
100,000th	one hundred thousandth
1,000,000th	one millionth
1,000,000,000th	one billionth

Days of the Week

Sunday
Monday
Tuesday
Wednesday
Thursday
Friday
Saturday

Months of the Year

January
February
March
April
May
June
July
August
September
October
November
December